WRITE

God

IN

JOURNAL YOUR WAY TO A DEEPER FAITH

 Sabrina McDonald

BARBOUR BOOKS
An Imprint of Barbour Publishing, Inc.

Written and compiled by Sabrina McDonald.

Print ISBN 978-1-68322-084-8

Published by Barbour Books, an imprint of Barbour Publishing, Inc., P.O. Box 719, Uhrichsville, Ohio 44683, www.barbourbooks.com.

Our mission is to publish and distribute inspirational products offering exceptional value and biblical encouragement to the masses.

 Member of the
Evangelical Christian
Publishers Association

Printed in China.

INTRODUCTION

Keep my commands and you will live;
guard my teachings as the apple of your eye.
Bind them on your fingers;
write them on the tablet of your heart.

PROVERBS 7:2–3 NIV

♥

Words have power. James declared, "How great a forest is set ablaze by such a small fire!" (3:5 ESV). Wars have been started by a single written letter. Other wars were won because of the strength of a provocative speech. Words—they can persuade, heal, and strengthen.

But there are words that are often neglected in our modern times—our own written words that testify how God has touched our lives, words in our own handwriting that can't be photoshopped or deleted from a server. These expressions pass down from one generation to the next as first-hand accounts of God's life-changing power.

Write God In is meant to be a handwritten process of feeding and flourishing the promises of God in your life. Second Peter 1:4 says, "[God] has granted to us his precious and very great promises, so that through them you may become partakers of the divine nature, having escaped from the corruption that is in the world" (ESV). God has provided a spiritual sanctuary, a place where you can eat the fruits of His garden—even in the midst of this barren world—just by understanding the scripture.

This book will usher you into that place, taking you through twenty-five promises of God's Word examining the scripture, your own heart, and the lives of women in the Bible and throughout history who exemplify these characteristics. These women will serve as mentors throughout your journey.

Before you begin, prepare your heart to receive a word of encouragement from the Lord. Spend some time on your knees, asking Him to bring you deeper into His presence. For you won't see fruition until you are firmly connected to the Source.

Now take up your pen and get ready to journal your way to a deeper faith.

WRITE PURPOSE INTO YOUR LIFE

Marilyn Monroe was known for saying, "Diamonds are a girl's best friend." But she forgot to mention that diamonds come at a great price, not only for the pocketbook, but for nature as well. Those indestructible beauties come from an incredible amount of pressure applied to carbon-containing minerals, and once the jewels are formed, they must be mined, cut, and polished.

Other precious gems and metals also develop under difficult circumstances. Gold is made pure with fire. Pearls are formed through the struggles of an agitated clam. The birthing process of precious stones and metals is never easy, but the outcome is exquisite.

In the same way, everyone longs to have the treasure of a fulfilled life—contentment, deep love, respect, wisdom—but those jewels often come as a result of great pressure, pain, and struggle.

When we go through turmoil, God is refining, teaching, and training our hearts and souls, and in the process, He's bringing about His purposes in our lives and in the lives of others through us.

Each struggle is a new jewel in the spiritual treasure trove of your destiny. Everything that happens to you has a purpose in bringing about the will of God. As He builds a testimony in you, you can build up others in the body of Christ. Together "we can comfort those in any trouble with the comfort we ourselves receive from God" (2 Corinthians 1:4 NIV).

In John 11, Martha's brother Lazarus was dying. She sent word to Jesus so He would come and heal her brother, but Jesus purposely stayed where He was so His beloved friend would die. When Jesus finally arrived, four days after Lazarus's death, Martha cried out, "If you had been here, my brother would not have died" (John 11:21 ESV). But Jesus had already told His disciples, "This illness does not lead to death. It is for the glory of God, so that the Son of God may be glorified" (John 11:4 ESV). You see, Jesus had a plan, one which He then executed—He raised Lazarus from the dead.

How do you identify with Martha? Make a list of all the ways God has used difficult situations in your life to bring about His glory.

St. luke 10:17   19:20
Life of Saluation gives you power over
Evil - You can turn from pride, hurting of others
Fashion, lying, Stealing, Cheating
1 Cor 6:9
Eph 6:
Col 3:5

Meditate on this scripture: "And we know that all things work together for good to them that love God, to them who are the called according to his purpose" (Romans 8:28 KJV).

What does this mean to you?

....

....

....

....

....

....

....

....

....

....

....

....

....

....

....

....

....

....

....

....

....

....

....

....

....

....

In her book *The Hiding Place*, Corrie ten Boom, a surviving prisoner of a Nazi concentration camp, wrote, "In darkness God's truth shines most clear."

What does this mean to you?

....
....
....
....
....
....
....
....
....
....
....
....
....
....
....
....
....
....
....
....
....
....
....
....
....
....

In Psalm 34:19 (NIV), David, the shepherd boy God made king, wrote, "The righteous person may have many troubles, but the LORD delivers him from them all."

List three ways adversity has been used for good in your life. Consider how God used these experiences to bring you closer to Him.

....

....

....

....

....

....

....

....

....

....

....

....

....

....

....

....

....

....

....

....

....

....

....

....

....

....

....

....

The Old Testament book of Esther is about a young Jewish girl who was chosen to marry the king because of her beauty. Once wed, she discovered a plot by one of the king's trusted advisors to eliminate her people, the Jews. Esther was caught in a difficult dilemma with her life on the line. She could have chosen to keep her ethnicity a secret, but instead, she listened to the words of her wise uncle, who said, "Who knows whether you have not come to the kingdom for such a time as this?" (Esther 4:14 ESV). Esther used her influence to save her people.

How does Esther's story inspire you?

In 2 Corinthians 9:8 (NIV), Paul, suffering with a thorn in his flesh, told readers, "God is able to bless you abundantly, so that in all things at all times, having all that you need, you will abound in every good work."

List any difficult situations in your life that you are currently experiencing, and consider how God may use these situations for His purpose.

In her book *A Path through Suffering*, Elisabeth Elliot wrote, "Each time the mystery of suffering touches us personally and all the cosmic questions arise fresh in our minds, we face the choice between faith (which accepts) and unbelief (which refuses to accept)."

Consider how you see this truth in your own life.

In 2 Corinthians 1:8–9 (NIV), Paul writes, "We do not want you to be uninformed, brothers and sisters, about the troubles we experienced in the province of Asia. . . . But this happened that we might not rely on ourselves but on God."

Write a prayer asking God to show you how He is planning to use your past or current suffering to accomplish great things through you. How is God speaking to you?

....

....

....

....

....

....

....

....

....

....

....

....

....

....

....

....

....

....

....

....

....

....

....

....

....

....

....

....

....

In Philippians 1:12 (NLT), Paul tells his readers, "I want you to know, my dear brothers and sisters, that everything that has happened to me here has helped to spread the Good News."

If you could start a ministry through your own experiences and testimony of God's work in your life, what would it be? Who would you reach? How would you encourage them?

....
....
....
....
....
....
....
....
....
....
....
....
....
....
....
....
....
....
....
....
....
....
....
....
....

♥2♥

WRITE SHELTER INTO YOUR LIFE

Margaret Hillis was a missionary in China during the Japanese invasion in 1941. When food ran out, God provided two visitors—one with milk, the other with eggs. As the gunfire grew louder, Margaret couldn't sleep. She prayed for deliverance. The next morning, all was quiet—the troops had mysteriously withdrawn.

Humans are fragile. It doesn't take much to stop a beating heart—a spider bite, an airborne germ, or an offended stranger. But God is impenetrable!

Psalm 27:3, 5 (ESV) explains it this way:

> *Though an army encamp against me, my heart shall not fear; though war arise against me, yet I will be confident. . . . For he will hide me in his shelter in the day of trouble; he will conceal me under the cover of his tent; he will lift me high upon a rock.*

But what about those who died for their faith or the child who wasn't healed? Our suffering has eternal purpose. Hebrews 12:11 (ESV) tells us, "For the moment all discipline seems painful rather than pleasant, but later it yields the peaceful fruit of righteousness to those who have been trained by it."

God sees your suffering, and you will be rewarded for it in heaven. The apostle Paul expresses this well in Romans 8:18 (ESV): "For I consider that the sufferings of this present time are not worth comparing with the glory that is to be revealed to us."

When at death God brings saints into their rest, it's because their job on earth is done. "Blessed are the dead who die in the Lord from now on. . . . They will rest from their labor, for their deeds will follow them" (Revelation 14:13 NIV). Death to the Christian is not a life taken—it is eternal life given!

Psalm 71:3, 5 (NLT) says, "Be my rock of safety where I can always hide. Give the order to save me, for you are my rock and my fortress. . . . O Lord, you alone are my hope. I've trusted you, O Lord, from childhood."

What difficult events in your life have brought you to a greater level of faith?

In Matthew 23:37 (ESV), Jesus said, "O Jerusalem, Jerusalem, the city that kills the prophets and stones those who are sent to it! How often would I have gathered your children together as a hen gathers her brood under her wings."

How does this imagery comfort you?

....

....

....

....

....

....

....

....

....

....

....

....

....

....

....

....

....

....

....

....

....

....

....

....

....

....

....

....

Psalm 91:9, 11–12 (NLT) says, "If you make the LORD your refuge, if you make the Most High your shelter. . .he will order his angels to protect you wherever you go. They will hold you up with their hands so you won't even hurt your foot on a stone."

When and how have you seen God's protection in your life?

....
....
....
....
....
....
....
....
....
....
....
....
....
....
....
....
....
....
....
....

Rahab was a harlot who helped the Israelites defeat Jericho. She had become a believer of the Jewish God, and she was prepared to put her life on the line for her faith. In the end she was protected and saved. More than that, she later experienced an identity transformation: from harlot to ancestor of Jesus. Her protection and salvation went beyond the physical to the spiritual. Read the full story in Joshua 2 and 6.

How does Rahab's story inspire you?

....

....

....

....

....

....

....

....

....

....

....

....

....

....

....

....

....

....

....

....

....

....

In 2 Kings 6:17 (NLT), the prophet Elisha, surrounded by enemy troops, asked God to show his panicking servant the reality of His power: "Elisha prayed, 'O Lord, open his eyes and let him see!' The Lord opened the young man's eyes, and when he looked up, he saw that the hillside around Elisha was filled with horses and chariots of fire."

What life events have caused you to question whether God was still with you? How did you feel when God opened your eyes to His presence?

....
....
....
....
....
....
....
....
....
....
....
....
....
....
....
....
....
....
....
....
....
....

In John 14:2 (NIV), Jesus says, "My Father's house has many rooms; if that were not so, would I have told you that I am going there to prepare a place for you?"

What about your future eternal life will be better than your life here on earth?

Even though Sarah and Abraham were promised a son by God, the aging Sarah assumed she was barren. So she told Abraham to lie with her servant Hagar, who bore a son named Ishmael. About fourteen years later, Sarah had a son by Abraham and named him Isaac. The jealous Sarah later demanded that Hagar and Ishmael be thrown out into the wilderness. Even though Hagar and her child were left to die, God protected them because of His mercy and His covenant with Abraham. Read the full story in Genesis 16 and 21.

How does this story show God's protection through mercy?

Teresa of Ávila said, "Christ has no body now but yours. No hands, no feet on earth but yours. Yours are the eyes through which he looks compassion on this world. Yours are the feet with which he walks to do good. Yours are the hands through which he blesses all the world."

In what ways can you help shelter and protect others by being our loving God's hands and feet?

....

....

....

....

....

....

....

....

....

....

....

....

....

....

....

....

....

....

....

....

....

In 2 Samuel 22:3–4 (ESV), a rescued David says to the Lord, "My God, my rock, in whom I take refuge, my shield, and the horn of my salvation, my stronghold and my refuge, my savior; you save me from violence. I call upon the LORD, who is worthy to be praised, and I am saved from my enemies."

Pray these verses from your own heart. What names for God would you add? What thoughts and feelings come up for you?

♥3♥

WRITE KINDNESS INTO YOUR LIFE

In 1997 more than twenty-five nations came together to form The World Kindness Movement, an organization created to "inspire individuals towards greater kindness and. . .create a kinder world."[1] In an article that appeared in *Timeless Spirit Magazine*, people today are described as "at war with. . .the neighbors' howling dog, rising prices, rude people, the noisy garbage truck, the promotion we didn't get, unruly children. . . . It seems as if humanity is going through some mid-life crisis."[2]

But we Christians don't need a movement. Scripture calls us to live with kindness at the forefront of our behavior. "Therefore, as God's chosen people, holy and dearly loved, clothe yourselves with compassion, kindness, humility, gentleness and patience" (Colossians 3:12 NIV). To be clothed with these qualities is to show them on the exterior—to wear them for everyone to see.

Kindness should be unconditional. Jesus tells us to love our enemies, do good to those who hate us, bless those who curse us, and pray for those who mistreat us (see Luke 6:27–28). The kindness we give isn't intended to make a better world necessarily, but rather to reflect the kindness that God has shown us.

Kindness isn't a superpower you have to muster up in your own strength. You have the Holy Spirit to help. As long as you are tending the garden of your relationship with the Lord, you will bear this fruit of the Spirit—even in times of annoyance and distress.

Swiss American psychiatrist Elisabeth Kübler-Ross once said, "People are like stained-glass windows. They sparkle and shine when the sun is out, but when the darkness sets in, their true beauty is revealed only if there is a light from within."

Your kindness to others is that outward beauty shining through from an inward light—the light of the world (see Matthew 5:14).

---

[1] http://www.theworldkindnessmovement.org/about-us/
[2] http://www.timelessspirit.com/NOV03/brian.shtml

Mother Teresa said, "There is hunger for ordinary bread, and there is hunger for love, for kindness, for thoughtfulness; and this is the great poverty that makes people suffer so much."

What ordinary acts can you do that would fill the hunger for kindness in those around you?

Meditate on this verse: "Be kind to one another, tenderhearted, forgiving one another, as God in Christ forgave you" (Ephesians 4:32 ESV).

Journal whatever thoughts or ideas come to mind.

In one of Jesus' parables, a Samaritan, seeing a wounded man, "bandaged his wounds, pouring on oil and wine. Then he put the man on his own donkey, brought him to an inn and took care of him" (Luke 10:34 NIV).

Write about a time when you received an act of kindness from someone in your life. What did it mean to you? How did it inspire you?

Hebrews 13:2 (NIV) says, "Do not forget to show hospitality to strangers, for by so doing some people have shown hospitality to angels without knowing it."

Have you ever considered that a stranger could be an angel? How does that possibility make you feel?

The Shunammite woman's life was changed when she showed kindness to the prophet Elisha, urging him to have a meal at her house. He then came by so often, she suggested to her husband that they set up guest quarters for Elisha. Impressed by her kindness, the man of God looked for a way to bless the couple and prayed that the childless woman would have a male heir.

Read the story in 2 Kings 4:8–37 and then reflect on what it teaches you about kindness.

....
....
....
....
....
....
....
....
....
....
....
....
....
....
....
....
....
....
....
....

The world says, "No good deed goes unpunished." This type of negative attitude not only goes against Jesus' mandates but destroys the propensity for kindness.

What are some of the attitudes in your life that could use a transformation? Write a prayer stating the specific attitude adjustments that would ultimately benefit you and others.

Sarah Osborn Benjamin was the wife of a young private in George Washington's army. Before battles she carried beef, bread, and coffee to the men. When Washington asked her if she was afraid of the cannonballs, she replied, "It would not do for the men to fight and starve, too."

Sarah is an example of the strength of kindness.
In what ways is your kindness stronger than fear?

The writer Anne Lamott wrote in *Bird by Bird: Some Instructions on Writing and Life*, "You don't always have to chop with the sword of truth. You can point with it, too."

Oftentimes tongues struggle to speak kindness. On one side of the page, make a list of the unkind words you may be using. Then, on the opposite side of the page, make a second list of encouraging and uplifting words you can use to replace the words in the first list.

Consider Proverbs 31:26 (ESV): "She opens her mouth with wisdom, and the teaching of kindness is on her tongue."

How are wisdom and kindness connected?

....

....

....

....

....

....

....

....

....

....

....

....

....

....

....

....

....

....

....

....

....

....

WRITE GENEROSITY INTO YOUR LIFE

An old proverb says, "What I kept, I lost; what I spent, I had; what I gave, I have." Generosity is a mystery, for the one who gives is the one who receives the blessing.

Nettie McCormick would agree. After marrying Cyrus McCormick, inventor of the mechanical reaper, Nettie and her husband gave to numerous Christian organizations and also established a Presbyterian seminary later renamed McCormick Theological Seminary. After her husband's death in 1884, Nettie was a multimillionaire. She said, "Yes, money is power. . .but I have always tried not to trust in it, but rather use it for the glory of my Master."

Altogether, Nettie gave eight million dollars (today's equivalent of over $160 million) to hospitals, schools, relief agencies, and Christian organizations. She also founded forty-six schools, supported D. L. Moody's campaigns, and built (among other things) a woman's clinic in Persia and a seminary in Korea.

Nettie found the secret to happiness: a life of purpose. She said, "Usefulness is the great thing in life—to do something for others leaves a sweeter odor than a life of pleasure."

We may not have millions like Nettie, but we can give from what we have. Remember the widow's two mites? What others saw as a trifle, Jesus perceived as a great treasure: "Truly, I tell you, this poor widow has put in more than all of them. For they all contributed out of their abundance, but she out of her poverty" (Luke 21:3–4 ESV).

Paul wrote these guidelines for the rich in the church: "Tell them to use their money to do good. They should be rich in good works and generous to those in need, always being ready to share with others" (1 Timothy 6:18 NLT).

Nettie was right—God did not give us what we have so that we could drive nice cars, live in big homes, and take expensive vacations. He has given us what we have to care for the poor and expand His kingdom. Nettie's checkbook reflected that. What does yours reflect?

Consider 2 Corinthians 9:7 (ESV): "Each one must give as he has decided in his heart, not reluctantly or under compulsion, for God loves a cheerful giver."

Take some moments to examine your own heart. Do you give regularly to your church? Why or why not? When you do give, do you give begrudgingly or cheerfully?

Jesus said, "Where your treasure is, there your heart will be also" (Matthew 6:21 NASB).

Review your spending over the last month or two. Where is your heart? What are some pleasures you could do without in order to give to God's work?

....
....
....
....
....
....
....
....
....
....
....
....
....
....
....
....
....
....
....
....
....
....

Proverbs 11:24–25 (ESV) says, "One gives freely, yet grows all the richer; another withholds what he should give, and only suffers want. Whoever brings blessing will be enriched, and one who waters will himself be watered."

Reflect on how this applies to your own life.

Someone once said, "You can't out-give God." In other words, no matter how much you give, God will take care of you.

What are some ways you can give? What are some Christian charities you are excited about? How can you be more actively involved in giving generously to your church?

Read Acts 5:1–11. Ananias and Sapphira were faithful followers of Christ, but when they lied to the Holy Spirit about their giving, they were confronted by Peter and immediately dropped dead.

God is serious about you being honest as you give. What are your motives as you give to your church, charities, or causes?

Lydia was a successful businesswoman in the early church. She sold purple cloth and owned a home large enough to host Paul and other out-of-town guests. Although not much is known about Lydia, what is known is that she used the resources she had to help the ministry, and her work was so integral to the Philippian church that she made the pages of scripture (see Acts 16:14–15).

What resources do you have that you could use for God's kingdom?

....

....

....

....

....

....

....

....

....

....

....

....

....

....

....

....

....

....

....

....

....

....

Dorcas was another great example of generosity in the early church. Acts 9:36 (NIV) says, "She was always doing good and helping the poor." The rest of the passage explains that she made clothing for widows.

What gifts and abilities do you have that you could use to help others? What resources do you already have that you could give or share with those in need?

In the novel *Any Minute*, written by Joyce Meyer and Deborah Bedford, the character Grandma Annie says, "It is impossible to be both selfish and happy."

In what areas of life have you been selfish?
Where have you been generous?

....
....
....
....
....
....
....
....
....
....
....
....
....
....
....
....
....
....
....
....
....
....
....
....

Mother Teresa said, "Let us not be satisfied with just giving money. Money is not enough, money can be got, but they need your hearts to love them."

What does this mean to you? How does this challenge you?

....

....

....

....

....

....

....

....

....

....

....

....

....

....

....

....

....

....

....

....

....

....

....

WRITE BEAUTY INTO YOUR LIFE

Michelangelo, a brilliant painter and master sculptor, said, "In every block of marble I see a statue as plain as though it stood before me, shaped and perfect in attitude and in action. I have only to hew away the rough walls that imprison the lovely apparition to reveal it to the other eyes as mine see it."

In the same way, God—our Creator—looks at each person's life and sees a masterpiece standing before Him, although others may see only a plain and pointless existence. The loveliness is there just waiting to be set free by the masterful hands of God.

It is said that beauty is in the eye of the beholder. In the case of God's people, the beauty is in *His* eyes. Where we see brokenness, He sees healing. Where we see failure, He sees redemption. Where we see pain, He sees purpose.

Ecclesiastes 3:11 (ESV) says that God "has made everything beautiful in its time." God is diligent to better His people. He is not content just to let us sit in the mediocre and mundane. All the work God does is perfect and complete, preparing us for a radiant glory that surpasses any beauty we have ever known.

Jesus said, "Why do you worry about clothes? See how the flowers of the field grow. They do not labor or spin. Yet I tell you that not even Solomon in all his splendor was dressed like one of these" (Matthew 6:28–29 NIV). When you focus on the kingdom of God and make your life about His glory, beauty naturally results—not because of what you have done, but because He has done it all.

Actress Audrey Hepburn, a fashion and beauty icon as well as a humanitarian, said, "The beauty of a woman is not in a facial mole, but true beauty in a woman is reflected in her soul. It is the caring that she lovingly gives, the passion that she knows."

What do your passions reveal about your true beauty?

It has been said that "a woman deserves no credit for her beauty at sixteen, but beauty at sixty is her own soul's doing."

What are you doing now to invest in your "future" inner beauty?

....
....
....
....
....
....
....
....
....
....
....
....
....
....
....
....
....
....
....
....
....
....

Consider Proverbs 31:30 (NIV): "Charm is deceptive, and beauty is fleeting; but a woman who fears the LORD is to be praised."

What steps can you take to make the praises you receive from others (including God) more a result of your inner rather than your outer beauty?

....
....
....
....
....
....
....
....
....
....
....
....
....
....
....
....
....
....
....
....
....

Ashley Smith said, "Life is full of beauty. Notice it. Notice the bumble bee, the small child, and the smiling faces. Smell the rain, and feel the wind."

Beauty is all around you. You just need to open your eyes to all the loveliness God has created. What tangible beauty do you see? What intangible beauty do you see? Who are the beautiful people in your life?

....
....
....
....
....
....
....
....
....
....
....
....
....
....
....
....
....
....
....
....
....
....
....

Maya Angelou said, "It is time for parents to teach young people early on that in diversity there is beauty and there is strength."

Everyone has the potential to become a masterpiece. What people in your life could use your words of encouragement, words that would help them view themselves as a beautiful work in progress?

As already quoted in chapter 3 of *Write God In*, Swiss American psychiatrist Elisabeth Kübler-Ross said, "People are like stained-glass windows. They sparkle and shine when the sun is out, but when the darkness sets in, their true beauty is revealed only if there is a light from within."

What habits and sins in your life are smudging up your stained-glass window? How can you wipe the panes clean and let God's light shine through your life?

....

....

....

....

....

....

....

....

....

....

....

....

....

....

....

....

....

....

....

....

Consider the words of Isaiah 61:1, 3 (NIV): "The Spirit of the Sovereign LORD is on me. . .to bestow on them a crown of beauty instead of ashes, the oil of joy instead of mourning, and a garment of praise instead of a spirit of despair."

How has God used the ugly circumstances of your life to create something beautiful?

....

....

....

....

....

....

....

....

....

....

....

....

....

....

....

....

....

....

....

In Deuteronomy 4:29 (ESV), Moses told God's people, "You will seek the LORD your God and you will find him, if you search after him with all your heart and with all your soul."

In what ways are you making God your primary focus, seeking His kingdom first in your life, and thus allowing His beauty to naturally result? If you feel you're falling short in this area, what can you do to change things up?

....

....

....

....

....

....

....

....

....

....

....

....

....

....

....

....

....

....

....

In her book *Walking on Water: Reflections on Faith and Art*, Madeleine L'Engle, author of *A Wrinkle in Time*, believed her job as a writer was to bring all people close to Christ, not with a blatant slap in the face, but "by showing them a light that is so lovely that they want with all their hearts to know the source of it."

How does this thought inspire you to show others the same lovely light?

♥6♥

WRITE PEACE INTO YOUR LIFE

"I Heard the Bells on Christmas Day," the carol based on Henry Wadsworth Longfellow's poem "Christmas Bells," tells of a journey to discovering peace. The song describes the depression of wars and hate, but it ends with a renewed hope: "Then pealed the bells more loud and deep: 'God is not dead, nor doth He sleep; the wrong shall fail, the right prevail, with peace on earth, good will to men.'"

Because of man's sinful nature, there has been strife since the beginning. But Jesus promised that peace is attainable through Him. In John 16:33 (ESV), He said, "I have said these things to you, that in me you may have peace. In the world you will have tribulation. But take heart; I have overcome the world."

It doesn't matter how many trials we face or what battles rage in our lives. Jesus has already overcome! He is waiting to restore all things, and He's using this time to draw more believers to Himself— even *through* the pain created by fighting and chaos.

The angel that announced the birth of Christ said, "Glory to God in the highest heaven, and on earth peace to those on whom his favor rests" (Luke 2:14 NIV). To that point, we were *enemies* with the Almighty, but Jesus was the peace treaty that God offered to man.

In your oftentimes chaotic, strife-filled world, there is a place of tranquility in a faith-filled heart. You can rest in complete confidence, for Jesus has said, "Peace I leave with you; my peace I give you. I do not give to you as the world gives. Do not let your hearts be troubled and do not be afraid" (John 14:27 NIV).

Philippians 4:6 (ESV) says, "Do not be anxious about anything, but in everything by prayer and supplication with thanksgiving let your requests be made known to God."

What things in your life have the potential to steal your peace? Describe those issues and take them to God, one by one.

....

....

....

....

....

....

....

....

....

....

....

....

....

....

....

....

....

....

....

....

....

....

In Philippians 4:7 (ESV), Paul tells his readers that if their worries are given up to God, then "the peace of God, which surpasses all understanding, will guard your hearts and your minds in Christ Jesus."

Have you experienced unexplainable peace in difficult situations in the past? How did God give you such a peace?

....

....

....

....

....

....

....

....

....

....

....

....

....

....

....

....

....

....

....

....

....

....

Martha was much like many other women. When she had a crowd at her house, she worried *a lot* about the details, but she was missing out on the bigger picture. Jesus said to her, "Martha, Martha. . .you are worried and upset about many things, but few things are needed—or indeed only one" (Luke 10:41–42 NIV).

What things in life cause you to worry?
How can you eliminate some of those worries?

Jesus said, "Blessed are the peacemakers, for they will be called children of God" (Matthew 5:9 NIV).

Are you a troublemaker or a peacemaker in your sphere of influence? Consider your words, thoughts, and attitudes. What changes might you need to make to become a greater peacemaker?

....
....
....
....
....
....
....
....
....
....
....
....
....
....
....
....
....
....
....
....
....
....

Matthew 15:21-28 tells the story of a Canaanite woman whose daughter was suffering from demon possession. Even though it was a social taboo for this woman to come to Jesus, she did anyway, knowing that He held the cure for her problem. Jesus tested her by initially pushing back, citing her religious and cultural status, but in determination she would not take "no" for an answer! He responded, "'Woman, you have great faith! Your request is granted.' And her daughter was healed at that moment" (Matthew 15:28 NIV).

What does the Canaanite woman's story teach you about prayer?

Consider Kathleen Partridge's "To the Future":

The past has its store of joys we remember,
The future is ours undefiled. . .
Let us carry our weigh with courage of men,
But proceed with the trust of a child.

How does this poem inspire you in regard to peace in your life?

....

....

....

....

....

....

....

....

....

....

....

....

....

....

....

....

....

....

....

....

....

....

....

....

....

....

In *A Man Called Peter*, Catherine Marshall wrote, "Often God has to shut a door in our face, so that He can subsequently open the door through which He wants us to go."

What doors has God opened for you? What doors were shut so that you could walk through the ones God wanted to open for you? What peace does that give you today?

In 2 Chronicles 20:6 (ESV), Jehoshaphat prays, "O LORD, God of our fathers, are you not God in heaven? You rule over all the kingdoms of the nations. In your hand are power and might, so that none is able to withstand you."

The key to peace in life is such confidence in the sovereignty of God. Why do you trust God? Consider other scriptures and your own testimony.

....
....
....
....
....
....
....
....
....
....
....
....
....
....
....
....
....
....
....
....
....
....
....
....

Someone once observed, "There is no place to hide a sin, without the conscience looking in!"

You will never have contentment or peace in your heart if you have unrepentant sin in your life. That burden will feel like a rock in your shoe—you may be walking with the Lord, but you are going to get blisters. If you are dealing with a lack of peace, consider if you have dealt with the sin in your life. Journal about this. Take responsibility for it, confess your sin, and ask for God's forgiveness.

WRITE CONTENTMENT INTO YOUR LIFE

Fanny Crosby lost her sight when she was six weeks old due to a doctor's careless treatment. But Fanny counted her blindness as a blessing. "It is not the things I've missed, or never had, which make me sorrowful. It is the things I have had in full measure in which I rejoice daily."

Fanny wrote over 1,000 poems and 8,000 songs, including the hymns "Blessed Assurance" and "Safe in the Arms of Jesus," reflecting her attitude of contentment. She could have lived mourning her disability and blaming circumstances but instead chose to embrace the blessings of her debility, which strengthened and helped her to focus on her talent.

The apostle Paul also learned the secret of contentment: "In any and every circumstance, I have learned the secret of facing plenty and hunger, abundance and need. I can do all things through him who strengthens me" (Philippians 4:12–13 ESV).

Contentment has little to do with the condition of your circumstances. When you live in the abundance of the Spirit of Christ, satisfaction with your lot in life is a natural byproduct.

When thoughts and feelings of discontentment arise, the first step to contentment is renewing your mind to God's way of thinking (see Romans 12:2). The second is to seek first the kingdom of God, knowing that when you do so, God will provide above and beyond all that you need (see Matthew 6:33). Christ promises that the Father already *knows* your needs—not just your physical needs, but your emotional and spiritual needs as well (see Matthew 6:32)—and will meet those needs in abundance. Not that you would have all the money and luxuries of this world, but rather all the abundance of an even greater life—an everlasting one (see John 10:10).

When tempted by discontentment, recondition your thinking. Consider in what ways you can you use your present circumstances for His glory.

In Ecclesiastes 1:8 (NLT), Solomon writes, "Everything is wearisome beyond description. No matter how much we see, we are never satisfied. No matter how much we hear, we are not content."

In what ways do you find yourself discontented with life?

....

....

....

....

....

....

....

....

....

....

....

....

....

....

....

....

....

....

....

....

....

....

Jesus said, "Take care, and be on your guard against all covetousness, for one's life does not consist in the abundance of his possessions" (Luke 12:15 ESV).

If life doesn't consist of the abundance of possessions, what does it consist of?

....

....

....

....

....

....

....

....

....

....

....

....

....

....

....

....

....

....

....

....

....

Louise Clappe helped her physician husband settle the West in a rough-and-tumble gold-mining camp. In her letters to her sister, she wrote, "Everybody ought to go to the mines, just to see how little it takes to make people comfortable in the world."

In what ways could losing all your possessions help you find contentment?

Consider Matthew 6:19–21 (ESV):

Do not lay up for yourselves treasures on earth, where moth and rust destroy and where thieves break in and steal, but lay up for yourselves treasures in heaven, where neither moth nor rust destroys and where thieves do not break in and steal. For where your treasure is, there your heart will be also.

What treasures do you have stored in heaven?

Eileen A. Soper wrote,

Lord, make me now
As happy as the field.
With flowers enriched . . .

Who or what are the flowers enriching the field of your life?
How do they not only make you content but happy?

Consider these words of Martha Washington: "The greater part of our happiness or misery depends upon our dispositions, and not upon our circumstances."

Your life's circumstances are continually changing. How can you be content where you are right now?

Consider this poem by Ella Wheeler Wilcox:

It's easy enough to be pleasant
  When life flows by like a song,
But the man worth while is the one who will smile,
  When everything goes dead wrong;
For the test of the heart is trouble,
  And it always comes with the years,
And the smile that is worth the praises of earth
  Is the smile that shines through tears.

When have you smiled through troubles and tears? In what ways have you found God's strength to remain content through thick and thin?

....
....
....
....
....
....
....
....
....
....
....
....
....
....
....
....

Jesus' mother Mary was the perfect example of a woman who understood contentment. She was humble and conscientious of her faith in God, and God blessed her for it.

Read Luke 1:46–55, which is called the Magnificat— Mary's song of praise. What elements of contentment do you see in this passage?

....

....

....

....

....

....

....

....

....

....

....

....

....

....

....

....

....

....

....

....

....

....

....

In 2 Corinthians 10:5 (NIV), Paul writes, "We take captive every thought to make it obedient to Christ."

In what ways can you take your thoughts captive when you begin to struggle with discontentment?

8

WRITE WISDOM INTO YOUR LIFE

Wisdom is a mystery. Have you ever tried to explain the concept to a child? It's difficult to define, but everyone knows when it's present. . .or lacking. The website WikiHow.com tries to give some answers. It lists thirteen steps to becoming wiser through experience, including suggestions such as trying new things, reading a variety of books, and learning from other wise people.

King Solomon, famous for his wisdom, had his own advice: "The beginning of wisdom is this: Get wisdom. Though it cost all you have, get understanding" (Proverbs 4:7 NIV). Solomon obviously thought it was worth the price.

But James gives us a faster plan. "If any of you lacks wisdom, you should ask God, who gives generously to all without finding fault, and it will be given to you" (James 1:5 NIV). James says real wisdom begins with prayer. Although you can try all the other methods you want, you will end up being nothing more than a human encyclopedia. But true wisdom comes from possessing spiritual understanding, and that comes from God alone.

Poet and biographer Hildegarde Hawthorne explains this phenomenon of God-given wisdom:

> *Sometimes, looking deep into the eyes of a child, you are conscious of meeting a glance full of wisdom. The child has known nothing yet but love and beauty—all this piled-up world knowledge you have acquired is unguessed at by him. And yet you meet this wonderful look that tells you in a moment more than all the years of experience have seemed to teach.*

Wisdom is not really a mystery at all but rather the fruit of your relationship with the Father. The more time you spend with Him, the more you become like Him. Wisdom is available to every Christian who desires it. Simply ask, and spend time with the one who gives it.

Ida Wells-Barnett was an African American school teacher and journalist in the late 1800s. Despite continuous death threats, she spoke out about the heinous and violent act of lynching. On her tombstone are these words: "She told the truth in words so stirring she forced the world to listen."

Although she had everything going against her, Ida was remembered for the way she used her words—with wisdom and power. How can you follow in Ida's footsteps?

....

....

....

....

....

....

....

....

....

....

....

....

....

....

....

....

....

....

....

....

....

....

Meditate on 1 Corinthians 1:25 (NIV): "For the foolishness of God is wiser than human wisdom, and the weakness of God is stronger than human strength."

When have you seen an example of this in your own life or the lives of others?

. . . .

. . . .

. . . .

. . . .

. . . .

. . . .

. . . .

. . . .

. . . .

. . . .

. . . .

. . . .

. . . .

. . . .

. . . .

. . . .

. . . .

. . . .

. . . .

. . . .

. . . .

. . . .

. . . .

Read James 1:5 (NIV) aloud: "If any of you lacks wisdom, you should ask God, who gives generously to all without finding fault, and it will be given to you."

Pray and ask God for the wisdom His Word promises.
Journal the ideas and thoughts that come to mind.

Read 2 Samuel 20:14–22 about the wise woman of Abel who saved an entire city.

What can you learn from this story? In what ways can you employ this wise woman's peacemaking methods during times of personal and national conflict?

....
....
....
....
....
....
....
....
....
....
....
....
....
....
....
....
....
....
....
....
....
....

Proverbs 4:6 (NIV) says, "Do not forsake wisdom, and she will protect you; love her, and she will watch over you."

In what ways might you increase in wisdom?

....

....

....

....

....

....

....

....

....

....

....

....

....

....

....

....

....

....

....

....

....

....

....

....

Meditate on James 3:17 (NIV): "But the wisdom that comes from heaven is first of all pure; then peace-loving, considerate, submissive, full of mercy and good fruit, impartial and sincere."

In what ways are these virtues of God's wisdom displayed in your life?

....
....
....
....
....
....
....
....
....
....
....
....
....
....
....
....
....
....
....
....
....

Proverbs 3:13 (ESV) says, "Blessed is the one who finds wisdom, and the one who gets understanding."

Name three wise women you know. Consider the attributes and daily attitudes they display. How does wisdom bless their lives?

Proverbs 14:1 (NIV) says, "The wise woman builds her house, but with her own hands the foolish one tears hers down."

In what ways can you use wisdom to build up your inner and outer house—spiritually, physically, emotionally, and mentally?

....
....
....
....
....
....
....
....
....
....
....
....
....
....
....
....
....
....
....
....
....
....
....
....
....
....
....

Bible teacher Kay Arthur wrote, "When you know what God says, what He means, and how to put His truths into practice, you will be equipped for every circumstance of life."

How have you seen this truth in your own life?

WRITE COMPASSION INTO YOUR LIFE

In 1842, England's people were starving, but Florence Nightingale and her young upper-class friends had plenty to eat. She wrote, "My mind is absorbed with the idea of the sufferings of man; it besets me behind and before. . . . All that the poets sing of the glories of the world seem to me untrue. All the people I see are eaten up with care of poverty or disease."

When Florence left potential marriage, wealth, and society behind so she could do good works for Christ in the world, her family was horrified. She could have remained a wealthy Christian and just prayed for the suffering. But instead, Florence chose to be among the people. As a result, she became one of the greatest influences on nursing in history.

The Latin root of the word *compassion* means "suffer with." Frederick Buechner wrote, "Compassion is the sometimes fatal capacity for feeling what it is like to live inside somebody else's skin. It's the knowledge that there can never really be any peace and joy for me until there is peace and joy finally for you too."

Compassion is not just feeling sorry for people but wanting to do something to alleviate their suffering. The apostle John encouraged us, "Dear children, let us not love with words or speech but with actions and in truth" (1 John 3:18 NIV). Our loving compassion is to be followed up by deeds. Jesus said He didn't come to be served but to serve, and we should emulate that (see John 13:17). And as we attend to others, He will attend to us (see Philippians 4:16–19).

When you find yourself experiencing tender moments of compassion for another, don't dismiss the feeling. Let it sink deep into your soul. Do all that you can to resolve the pain to which God has opened your eyes and your heart. Let your compassion move you to love in action.

Galatians 6:9 (ESV) says, "And let us not grow weary of doing good, for in due season we will reap, if we do not give up."

Have you ever grown "weary of doing good"?
In what ways can you gain strength to carry on?

Read the story of the Good Samaritan in Luke 10:25–37.

*How does this story inspire you toward having
a compassionate heart?*

....
....
....
....
....
....
....
....
....
....
....
....
....
....
....
....
....
....
....
....
....
....
....
....
....

Emily Dickinson's poem "If I Can Stop One Heart from Breaking" captures the essence of compassion:

If I can stop one heart from breaking,
I shall not live in vain;
If I can ease one life the aching,
Or cool one pain,
Or help one fainting robin
Unto his nest again,
I shall not live in vain.

Write a prayer asking God to open your heart, mind, ears, and eyes to whom you can show compassion today, even if it's simply a smile to a sad or lonely person. Come back to your journal later today and record your experience.

First Peter 4:10 (ESV) says, "As each has received a gift, use it to serve one another, as good stewards of God's varied grace."

What gifts has God given you? Consider ways you can use your gifts in compassionately serving others.

Consider Alice Cary's poem "Nobility":

True worth is in being, not seeming,
In doing, each day that goes by
Some little good, not in dreaming
Of great things to do by and by.

What is "some little good" that you have done today?

Harriet Tubman escaped from slavery, but she wasn't satisfied with just her own freedom. Her family and friends were still enslaved, and she couldn't rest until she freed all of them, even when the pressure on runaway slaves was intensifying. "I was free, and they should be free," she said. Harriet Tubman eventually saved seventy enslaved family members and friends through her Underground Railroad, earning her the name Moses because her heart's desire was to lead her people to freedom.

Harriet's compassion was strengthened by her understanding of slavery. How have your personal struggles given you greater understanding?

Matthew 9:36 (NIV) says this about Jesus: "When he saw the crowds, he had compassion on them, because they were harassed and helpless, like sheep without a shepherd."

Write about a time when someone showed you compassion. Perhaps it was an unexpected helping hand, a shoulder to cry on, or an unforeseen kindness. How did the experience make you feel? How did it change your life?

After teaching in Calcutta, Mother Teresa became increasingly distressed by the poverty, hunger, and violence there, so she left her life at the convent and went to India, where she could minister among the poor and sick. She once said, "People are unrealistic, illogical, and self-centered. Love them anyway."

In what ways can you show love to the unlovable?

In Isaiah 58:7–8 (NLT), God said, "Share your food with the hungry, and give shelter to the homeless. Give clothes to those who need them, and do not hide from relatives who need your help. Then your salvation will come like the dawn, and your wounds will quickly heal. Your godliness will lead you forward, and the glory of the Lord will protect you from behind."

Write a prayer asking God to give you a heart of compassion with the wisdom to see the pain in others, the tenderness to feel the hurt, and the courage to take action to help promote healing. Then take a moment to listen to God's answer. Journal about any feelings, ideas, or thoughts that come to the fore.

♥ 10 ♥

WRITE CONFIDENCE INTO YOUR LIFE

Actress Loretta Young said, "A charming woman. . .doesn't follow the crowd. She is herself." For the Christian woman, we might change this slightly to say, "She is herself in Christ."

All women struggle with insecurities. By the world's standards, women are to be flawless. They are expected to earn high incomes, raise perfect children, make organic meals from scratch, look (and smell) attractive, and still have time for a life of fun and ease while doting on their husband, children, friends, and neighbors.

Impossible to achieve? Yes! But here's the good news—women don't have to live up to that standard. Their ultimate judge is God, and He has already provided all they need *in Christ alone.*

God has given us the blessed Holy Spirit to guide us through the decisions we make. And even when we aren't sure if those decisions are the best for everyone, we can be at peace, knowing God has sovereign control. We can trust Him to make the best of things—even our unintentional mistakes.

We don't need to compare ourselves to others. God's will for one life is likely not the same for another, and that's what makes God such a loving Father. He has a custom-made plan for each woman—and it is *always* a perfect fit.

So when you are faced with difficult choices, pray, consult the Bible, seek trusted godly counsel, and then make a decision, trusting God with the outcome. That's living life by God's standards. And as Isaiah 32:17 (NIV) says, "The fruit of that righteousness will be peace; its effect will be quietness and confidence forever."

Don't let the world, with its impossible standard of mass, cookie-cutter conformity, keep you in chains of anxiety. Seek the will of God alone, and stand confident in Him.

Mary Ann Bickerdyke volunteered as a nurse during the Civil War. When a surgeon once questioned who she was and what she was doing there, her response was, "I have received my authority from the Lord God Almighty. Have you anything that ranks higher than that?"

*In what way is God calling you to a great ministry—
one that might make others question your authority?*

Hebrews 13:6 (ESV) assures us that "we can confidently say, 'The Lord is my helper; I will not fear; what can man do to me?'"

How does this verse instill confidence in your soul?

....
....
....
....
....
....
....
....
....
....
....
....
....
....
....
....
....
....
....
....
....
....

What are the gifts and qualities God has given you? How might you use them to accomplish His purposes? What feelings come up when you consider that God will "equip you with everything good for doing his will" (Hebrews 13:21 NIV)?

God encouraged Joshua, the new leader of His people, saying, "Have I not commanded you? Be strong and courageous. Do not be frightened, and do not be dismayed, for the LORD your God is with you wherever you go" (Joshua 1:9 ESV).

These same words apply to you. Be courageous. Do not be frightened. Do not be dismayed. How could your life change if you did—with confidence—what the Lord commanded you?

....

....

....

....

....

....

....

....

....

....

....

....

....

....

....

....

....

....

....

....

Deborah was a prophetess, a wife, and a judge of Israel. It was rare for a woman to lead God's people, but the men had stumbled as leaders. When her people were being oppressed by their enemy, Deborah confronted her general, Barak, to find out why he hadn't taken the men into battle. But Barak's faith was weak, and he said he would only go if Deborah accompanied him. Barak looked only at the circumstances, but Deborah's confidence came from her faith in God. Even though the situation looked bleak to Barak, Israel won the battle (see Judges 4).

How does Deborah's story inspire you?

Before leading faithful singers to face great armies coming against his people, King Jehoshaphat encouraged them by saying, "Believe in the LORD your God, and you will be able to stand firm. Believe in his prophets, and you will succeed" (2 Chronicles 20:20 NLT).

Write about a time when you stood up for what was right while being opposed by others. If you haven't had such an experience, write about someone you admire who rose up amid opposition. What can you do to continue or begin to grow in confidence?

....
....
....
....
....
....
....
....
....
....
....
....
....
....
....
....
....

Consider these verses: "No one will be able to stand against you all the days of your life. As I was with Moses, so I will be with you; I will never leave you nor forsake you. Be strong and courageous" (Joshua 1:5–6 NIV).

Now write a prayer asking God to give you the boldness to stand for Him—in opposition to today's culture, perhaps even in the face of adversity.

In 2 Corinthians 12:9 (NLT), Paul writes that, when faced with affliction, Jesus told him, "My grace is all you need. My power works best in weakness."

Make a list of your insecurities. Compare that list to God's Word in Psalms 18 or 91. How does God's Word and Christ's presence give you strength in your weaknesses?

....

....

....

....

....

....

....

....

....

....

....

....

....

....

....

....

....

....

....

....

....

....

....

Amy Carmichael was a dedicated missionary in Asia. In *Gold Cord: The Story of a Fellowship*, she wrote, "My Confidence: Thou art able to keep that which I have committed unto Thee."

In what areas of life are you lacking confidence in God alone?
Consider changing things up by trusting God with the outcome
in every decision you make and action you take.

11

WRITE INTIMACY INTO YOUR LIFE

There's not a more intimate relationship than a monogamous marriage between husband and wife. The physical act of intimacy is an outward expression of completion, like two puzzle pieces that fit together perfectly.

For this reason, God chose marriage to reflect His covenant with His people. Paul makes it clear in Ephesians 5:31–32 (ESV): "'A man shall leave his father and mother and hold fast to his wife, and the two shall become one flesh.' This mystery is profound, and I am saying that it refers to Christ and the church."

We see examples of such intimacy throughout the Bible, but none is expressed so beautifully than the poetic illustration of Solomon and the Shulamite woman in the Song of Solomon. The two admire each other's outward appearance and inward character. Despite the woman's insecurities (see Song of Solomon 1:6; 3:1–4), Solomon finds her irresistible. In response, the Shulamite woman declares her eternal vow:

> *Place me like a seal over your heart, like a seal on your arm; for love is as strong as death, its jealousy unyielding as the grave. It burns like blazing fire, like a mighty flame. Many waters cannot quench love; rivers cannot sweep it away.* (SONG OF SOLOMON 8:6–8 NIV)

God knows our deepest inward parts, the places that not even a spouse knows. He knows our desires, intentions, and secret sins. He also knows who He created, who He intended us to be, and who we are becoming. He knows our struggles and failures, and yet He loves us just as we are.

There is not a man on earth who could satisfy your every intimate need or desire or accept you so wonderfully as you are. Yet God placed this longing in your heart so you would search for and find true completion and satisfaction in Him alone. His left arm is under your head while His right arm embraces you, gathering you, securing you in His presence, the place you always belong (see Song of Solomon 8:3). As unworthy as you are, God has invited you into His inner chamber. Enter in.

Consider Psalm 24:7 (NIV): "Lift up your heads, you gates; be lifted up, you ancient doors, that the King of glory may come in."

Do you feel like you have ever entered into the personal chambers of God? If not, what gets in the way of you joining Him?

Psalm 86:5–6 (ESV) says, "For you, O Lord, are good and forgiving, abounding in steadfast love to all who call upon you. Give ear, O LORD, to my prayer; listen to my plea for grace."

Make a list of all the things in your life that make you feel ashamed or unworthy. How does your perception of them keep you from getting close to God? If you regret these things and have confessed them, have you embraced God—and His forgiveness? What will you give up to get more of God?

The Shulamite woman declares, "[My lover] brought me to the banqueting house, and his banner over me was love" (Song of Solomon 2:4 ESV).

In the days of Solomon, banners were often used to declare the tribe of a household and to guide soldiers during war. But Solomon loves this woman so much that his entire household has turned from a symbol of bloodline and battle to one of tender guardianship and pure love. How does this reflect God's protection and love for you?

The Song of Solomon takes place, at one point, in a garden—reflecting the relationship of Adam and Eve before the fall. In the garden, the man and woman were "naked and were not ashamed" (Genesis 2:25 NASB), showing their absolute acceptance and freedom to be with one another in complete confidence.

You have this same kind of spiritual freedom with God. How does this inspire you?

....
....
....
....
....
....
....
....
....
....
....
....
....
....
....
....
....
....
....
....
....
....

In the Jewish temple, there was a heavy, thick veil or curtain that set apart the Holy of Holies—the inner sanctum where God dwelled. The only person allowed to enter that room was the high priest—the holiest person among the Jews—and he could only enter once a year to make a sacrifice on behalf of the people. But when Jesus died, an invisible power tore the veil from top to bottom (see Matthew 27:51), removing the manmade barriers between God and His people.

What feelings come up as you consider the extreme measures God took to draw you closer to Him and His love?

....

....

....

....

....

....

....

....

....

....

....

....

....

....

....

....

....

....

The Samaritan woman at the well had tried to find love in all the wrong places. She had had five husbands, and she was living with another man at the time of this encounter. But Jesus was the first man she ever met who knew everything she had ever done—and loved her anyway. For the first time in her life, she experienced true intimacy.

Read the full story in John 4:7–30.
What does this tell you about the love of Christ?

....
....
....
....
....
....
....
....
....
....
....
....
....
....
....
....
....
....
....
....
....
....

James 4:8 (ESV) says, "Draw near to God, and he will draw near to you."

What can you do to draw near to God?

Consider these words from Ethel Romig Fuller's poem "Proof":

If radio's slim fingers can pluck a melody
From night, and toss it over a continent or sea;
If the petaled white notes of a violin
Are blown across the mountains or the city's din;
If songs, like crimson roses, are culled from thin blue air—
Why should mortals wonder if God hears prayer?

Although you cannot see or touch God, in what ways do you know that He is very near and hears your pleas and praises?

....
....
....
....
....
....
....
....
....
....
....
....
....
....
....
....
....
....
....

Meditate on Song of Solomon 8:3 (ESV): "His left hand is under my head, and his right hand embraces me!"

*Enter the intimacy of God's presence and ask Him
to draw you nearer. Record your prayer here:*

• 12 •

WRITE POWER INTO YOUR LIFE

Several years ago, British researchers conducted a door-to-door survey asking about personal beliefs in the character of God. One question asked, "Do you believe in a God who intervenes in human history, who changes the course of affairs, who performs miracles, etc.?"[3] One man's response seemed to sum up their findings: "No, I don't believe in that God; I believe in the ordinary God."[4]

Many people in the Western church reflect this sentiment. They see God as they see themselves—powerless. But their thinking is skewed. The truth is that God, the maker of heaven and earth, has limitless power. And He has given you that power to overcome all unrighteousness, to speak with authority by the Word of God, and to bring light into the darkness and point the way for the lost.

When you fill your mind with scripture, it becomes a fountain of living water, spilling out on those around you. You will see spiritual gardens begin to grow as you live and share—not because of what you've done, but because the Spirit is at work.

Having the power of the Holy Spirit does not mean your life will be perfect—you can't have a testimony without trials, failures, and flaws. But it does mean you will be filled with purpose. The apostle Paul knew the struggles of imperfection and weakness. He prayed that God would remove a part of his life that troubled him, but the Lord refused, saying, "My grace is sufficient for you, for my power is made perfect in weakness" (2 Corinthians 12:9 NIV).

The Christian life was meant to be lived with an inner strength. You don't have to go into the fray alone and unprepared. The Holy Spirit is with you, providing the power He possesses and the discipline to prepare for the battle.

---

[3] Al Mohler, *Words from the Fire: Hearing the Voice of God in the Ten Commandments* (Chicago: Moody Publishers, 2009), 38.
[4] Ibid.

Perpetua was one of the early Christians and one of the first martyrs. She was young and had an infant child, and her beloved father begged her to recant her faith because he knew she would be thrown to wild beasts, forced to suffer until she died. But she refused, telling him, "It will all happen in the prisoner's dock as God wills, for you may be sure that we are not left to ourselves but are all in his power." Perpetua underwent great pains as she was beaten, watched her father beaten, and agonized as her infant child nearly starved, but she would not deny Christ and even came before her accusers singing psalms and walking confidently into the area where she would die.

How do you see supernatural power in Perpetua's life?
How does she inspire you?

Luke tells us the story of a woman with a bleeding disorder (see Luke 8:43—48). When Jesus walked through a crowd, she reached out and touched just the hem of His garment, and immediately she was healed. Jesus felt the power leave His body and said, "Who was it that touched me?" (Luke 8:45 ESV). The woman acknowledged her action, and Jesus said, "Daughter, your faith has made you well; go in peace" (Luke 8:48 ESV).

This woman knew where to go for the power to be made well. What are ways you can reach out, touch Jesus, and experience His power through faith?

Read and meditate on these verses:

- "God gave us a spirit not of fear but of power and love and self-control" (2 Timothy 1:7 ESV).

- "Finally, be strong in the Lord and in the strength of his might" (Ephesians 6:10 ESV).

- "[May you be] strengthened with all power, according to his glorious might, for all endurance and patience with joy" (Colossians 1:11 ESV).

Which verse speaks the most to your heart?
Journal the thoughts and feelings that come up for you.

....

....

....

....

....

....

....

....

....

....

....

....

....

....

....

Second Corinthians 13:4 (ESV) says, "For he was crucified in weakness, but lives by the power of God. For we also are weak in him, but in dealing with you we will live with him by the power of God." Consider Christians in your life who have confidence in the power of God. These may be fellow church members or people in your family.

What do you think gave them their strength?
How can you live the same kind of life?

....

....

....

....

....

....

....

....

....

....

....

....

....

....

....

....

....

....

....

The apostle Paul said, "I was with you in weakness and in fear and much trembling, and my speech and my message were not in plausible words of wisdom, but in demonstration of the Spirit and of power, so that your faith might not rest in the wisdom of men but in the power of God" (1 Corinthians 2:3–5 ESV).

What are your weaknesses? What are some ways that God can use His power through your weaknesses so that He can be glorified?

....

....

....

....

....

....

....

....

....

....

....

....

....

....

....

....

....

Consider the words of Psalm 73:26 (NLT): "My health may fail, and my spirit may grow weak, but God remains the strength of my heart; he is mine forever."

What are the ways God is calling you to serve Him even though your weaknesses? How can you step out in faith to minister to others even when it's difficult?

Jesus said, "With man this is impossible, but with God all things are possible" (Matthew 19:26 NIV).

In the past, how has God shown you His power through seemingly impossible circumstances?

In 2 Timothy 3:5, Paul tells his readers to avoid people who have the appearance of holiness but deny its power.

Do you have people like that in your life? How are they being deceived? How can you pray for them?

....

....

....

....

....

....

....

....

....

....

....

....

....

....

....

....

....

....

....

....

....

....

....

....

In Acts 1:8 (NLT), Jesus said, "You will receive power when the Holy Spirit comes upon you. And you will be my witnesses, telling people about me everywhere."

Write a prayer asking God to help you live a life that flows with the power of the Holy Spirit and shines the light of the Gospel through every word and action.

♥ 13 ♥

WRITE GRATITUDE INTO YOUR LIFE

Many Christians have proudly chanted, "God is good all the time! All the time, God is good!" While those statements are true, they seem to be said only after some great victory. For once it would be nice to hear them proclaimed after a great tragedy—because even then, God is still good!

Gratitude is difficult in the dark. Although it's easy to say, "Thank you, Lord!" when the sun is shining and everything appears easy, thanksgiving leaves a bitter taste in the mouth just after digesting discouragement. Giving sincere thanks amid tragedy is hard, but it's possible.

Poet Phillis Wheatley is a great example. Born in Africa, she was sold into slavery at around age seven and arrived in America skinny, naked, and sickly. She was bought by John and Susanna Wheatley, who treated her like a family member, seeing to her Christian education and baptism. She penned these remarkable words:

> 'Twas mercy brought me from my Pagan land
> Taught my benighted soul to understand
> That there's a God, that there's a Saviour too:
> Once I redemption neither sought nor knew.

Phillis saw past the villainy of enslavement to the sovereign plan of God to reach her with His love and mercy, even through such monstrous circumstances.

Besides giving thanks for what God *has* done, you can give thanks in faith for what God *will* do, what He has promised in the future. Romans 8:28 (NASB) says, "God causes all things to work together for good to those who love God, to those who are called according to His purpose." You can trust God's Word. Even though you can't see the end of the road, if you stay on God's path, it will eventually lead you to a land flowing with milk and honey. Although you may only sometimes catch momentary glimpses of the promised land today, you can thank God now—in faith—that what He promises He will fulfill tomorrow.

Psalm 105:1 (ESV) says, "Oh give thanks to the LORD; call upon his name; make known his deeds among the peoples!"

Write about all the ways God has done great deeds for you, and write a prayer thanking Him for them!

In Luke 17:11-19, Jesus heals ten lepers, but only one returns to thank Him. Commenting upon this in her book *Lessons I Learned in the Dark*, Jennifer Rothschild wrote, "May we all be like the one, rather than the nine."

Do you know any grateful people? What characteristics define these people's lives and behaviors? How do they inspire you?

Psalm 43:5 (KJV) says, "Why art thou cast down, O my soul? and why art thou disquieted within me? hope in God: for I shall yet praise him, who is the health of my countenance, and my God."

Think of the difficult circumstances you are going through. How can you give thanks to God in faith for what He has promised to do in the future? Write a prayer and thank Him now.

Washington Irving said, "Those who do not weep, do not see."[5]

How does this quote encourage you?

....
....
....
....
....
....
....
....
....
....
....
....
....
....
....
....
....
....
....
....
....
....
....
....
....

---

[5] Russ Kick, ed., *Quotes That Will Change Your Life: A Curated Collection of Mind-Blowing Wisdom* (Plum Island Books, 2015), 147.

In *Just Give Me Jesus*, Anne Graham Lotz writes, "One way to drive Satan to distraction, and to overcome him, is through praise of Jesus."

What tests and trials in your past has God used to bring about good in your life? Thank Him specifically for each blessing.

Elsie Janis's poem "Compensation" ends with this stanza:

When I think of the hundreds of things I might be,
I get down on my knees and thank God that I'm me.
Then my blues disappear, when I think what I've got,
And quite soon I've forgotten the thing I have not.

List some of the things you might be. Journal your
gratefulness to God for the things you are glad you are not.

....
....
....
....
....
....
....
....
....
....
....
....
....
....
....
....
....
....
....
....
....
....

Hebrews 13:15 (ESV) says, "Through him then let us continually offer up a sacrifice of praise to God, that is, the fruit of lips that acknowledge his name."

Sometimes gratitude can be a sacrifice. How can you offer gratitude to God, even if it comes at a great cost?

Luke 7:36–50 tells the story of a sinful woman who was so grateful for the love of Jesus that she bowed before Him, washed His feet with her tears, and then wiped them with her hair. She then took her most precious possession—a vile of expensive perfume—and used it to anoint His feet. This woman spoke no words. She didn't fear the gossip of those who despised her. She simply took action because the love and the gratefulness in her heart compelled her to lavish adoration on Jesus.

Have you ever felt as grateful to Jesus as this woman? Do you hope to?

....

....

....

....

....

....

....

....

....

....

....

....

....

....

....

....

....

....

....

....

....

In *Be Still My Soul*, Elisabeth Elliot writes, "God never does anything to us that isn't for us."

One of the ways you can show gratitude to God is to tell others about what He's done in your life—to share your testimony. What has God done for you in the past that you can share with others?

♥ 14 ♥

WRITE JOY INTO YOUR LIFE

You can't cut off an apple tree from its roots and expect to grow apples. You can't take away water and nutrients from a tomato plant and still expect to get tomatoes. But when a plant is getting everything it needs, it can't help but produce fruit because it's in the nature of the plant to do so.

It's the same way with the fruits of the Spirit. When you are connected to the vine of Jesus, joy will be one of the results because that is the nature of the Holy Spirit that then dwells within you.

Nehemiah 8:10 (NIV) says, "The joy of the LORD is your strength." In his commentary pertaining to this verse, Matthew Henry insightfully states, "Holy joy will be the oil to the wheels of our obedience." In other words, the joy we feel in our hearts makes the Word of the Lord easier to submit to and accomplish.

Jesus came to bring you this joy. Isaiah 61:3 (NIV) proclaims that the Messiah will bestow "the oil of joy instead of mourning, and a garment of praise instead of a spirit of despair." You no longer have to walk in sorrow because of your sin and shame. Jesus has brought reconciliation for you. You no longer have to fear the destruction of your soul. You now have one who will deliver you, and you can establish your joy in Him—not in your circumstances, the people in your life, or your accomplishments.

When everything around you seems to be falling apart, you can still have joy because the perfect kingdom of God is still to come and you can place your hope in that!

In *As Silver Refined*, Kay Arthur wrote, "No matter what happens, beloved, no matter how disappointing it is, you must first, in act of the will, rejoice and pray and give thanks."

What are some difficult circumstances in your life in which you can, as an act of the will, rejoice, pray, and give thanks?

Amy Carmichael wrote, "A cup brimful of sweetness cannot spill even one drop of bitter water, no matter how suddenly jarred."

How does this statement challenge and inspire you?

Leah was the unfavorite wife of Jacob. She birthed many sons to try to catch her husband's attention, hoping every time to gain his love. Then she gave birth to the son she named Judah, saying, "This time I will praise the Lord" (Genesis 29:35 NIV). Leah chose to praise the Lord and have joy in Him despite her circumstances. What she didn't know was that this line of Judah would eventually lead to Jesus, who would be our everlasting joy.

What can you learn from Leah's story?

Jesus said, "Until now you have asked nothing in my name. Ask, and you will receive, that your joy may be full" (John 16:24 ESV).

What requests do you need to bring to God?
Why not do so now and realize the fullness of joy?

Proverbs 10:28 (ESV) says, "The hope of the righteous brings joy."

Write about the ways you find strength in the joy of the Lord in your own life.

In *The Power of a Positive Woman*, Karol Ladd wrote, "Joy is more than a feeling; it is a deep peace, blended together with a solid hope that God has not left us. Joy is a delight in knowing there will be a better day. Can we have joy as our companion even when the road gets bumpy? Absolutely."

Think about the Christian women in your life who seem to have unwavering joy no matter their circumstances. How do they inspire you?

James 1:2–4 (ESV) says, "Count it all joy, my brothers, when you meet trials of various kinds, for you know that the testing of your faith produces steadfastness. And let steadfastness have its full effect, that you may be perfect and complete, lacking in nothing."

How have you seen this truth in your own life?

In John 15:5 (NIV), Jesus said, "I am the vine; you are the branches. If you remain in me and I in you, you will bear much fruit; apart from me you can do nothing."

How can you stay connected to the vine?
What are practical steps you can take to nurture
your spiritual roots?

Proverbs 31 describes a virtuous woman, who is an example for all women to follow. Verse 25 (ESV) says, "She laughs at the time to come." This woman doesn't have fear and anxiety when she looks at her future, but she trusts God and goes forward with joy.

How does she encourage you?

....
....
....
....
....
....
....
....
....
....
....
....
....
....
....
....
....
....
....
....
....
....

WRITE JUSTICE INTO YOUR LIFE

King Solomon had a difficult decision—two women claimed to be the mother of the same baby. How would he distinguish the real mother? The wise king ordered the baby cut in half so they could both have part, but one woman cried, "No! Give the baby to her, but only do not kill him" (see 1 Kings 3:27). Then Solomon knew who the real mother was.

God loves justice, and He calls us to love it. "Learn to do good; seek justice, correct oppression; bring justice to the fatherless, plead the widow's cause" (Isaiah 1:17 ESV). Christians should be known as those who pay and charge fairly, help those in need, and give generously. The Golden Rule still applies today: "Do to others what you would have them do to you" (Matthew 7:12 NIV).

Living justly also means extending forgiveness. In May 2016, a Christian woman in Iraq was told by Islamic State of Iraq and Syria (ISIS) fighters to leave her home or pay taxes. The woman told them, "I will pay. Give me a few seconds; my daughter is in the shower." Not willing to wait, the fighters torched the house. Although mother and daughter escaped their home, the severely burned daughter later died in the hospital in her mother's arms. Her last words were, "Forgive them."

You are to love your enemies the same way God loved you when you were *His* enemy. Despite your nature to reject Him, Jesus died in your place.

Even though God's mercy is deep and His patience long, evil will not ultimately go unpunished. Jesus said in Luke 18:7–8 (ESV), "Will not God give justice to his elect, who cry to him day and night? . . . I tell you, he will give justice to them speedily." In the end, all debts will be paid, for God says, "It is mine to avenge; I will repay" (Deuteronomy 32:35 NIV). You can trust God to have justice where there is evil, but best of all, you can trust Him to have mercy.

In *When Bad Things Happen to Good People*, Kay Arthur wrote, "No cruelty, no crime, no injustice escapes the attention of God."

Have you or a close friend ever been a victim of or witness to injustice? What lessons did you learn from the experience?

Jesus said, "You have heard that it was said, 'An eye for an eye and a tooth for a tooth.' But I say to you, Do not resist the one who is evil. But if anyone slaps you on the right cheek, turn to him the other also" (Matthew 5:38–39 ESV).

How does this passage challenge you?

In *Beautiful Girlhood*, Mabel Hale wrote, "Honesty or dishonesty is shown in every little act of life."

In what small ways can you make changes in your life to be more just in your living? Do you disobey traffic laws, cheat to get something better for yourself, or tell little white lies?
Small changes can make a big difference.

James 4:1–2 (ESV) says, "What causes quarrels and what causes fights among you? Is it not this, that your passions are at war within you? You desire and do not have, so you murder. You covet and cannot obtain, so you fight and quarrel. You do not have, because you do not ask."

How does this apply to your life? How does it apply to today's culture?

....
....
....
....
....
....
....
....
....
....
....
....
....
....
....
....
....
....
....
....
....
....
....

Corrie ten Boom survived one of the worst Nazi concentration camps in the Second World War. Many years later, one of her guards became a Christian and reached out to shake her hand after hearing her testimony. Corrie felt the rage and revenge surge through her in that moment, but she began to pray and, miraculously, feelings of love and forgiveness started welling up inside her. She wrote about this moment in *The Hiding Place*: "When [God] tells us to love our enemies, He gives us along with the command, the love itself."

How does this story inspire you?

Read John 8:1–11. A woman was caught in the act of adultery. Her accusers were ready to stone her, but Jesus told them, "Let him who is without sin among you be the first to throw a stone at her" (John 8:7 ESV).

Have you ever felt like repaying someone for his or her wrongs against you? If so, how does this passage challenge you?

. . . .

. . . .

. . . .

. . . .

. . . .

. . . .

. . . .

. . . .

. . . .

. . . .

. . . .

. . . .

. . . .

. . . .

. . . .

. . . .

. . . .

. . . .

. . . .

. . . .

Consider the words of Psalm 103:8 (ESV): "The LORD is merciful and gracious, slow to anger and abounding in steadfast love."

How can you have more mercy in your life based on the mercy God has given you?

Romans 12:19 (ESV) says, "Beloved, never avenge yourselves, but leave it to the wrath of God, for it is written, 'Vengeance is mine, I will repay, says the Lord.'"

How does it comfort and convict you that God will bring justice to all wrong in the end?

Consider Jeremiah 9:24 (ESV): "Let him who boasts boast in this, that he understands and knows me, that I am the LORD who practices steadfast love, justice, and righteousness in the earth. For in these things I delight, declares the LORD."

How can you trust God to judge the world?
What do you know about His righteousness?

....

....

....

....

....

....

....

....

....

....

....

....

....

....

....

....

....

....

....

....

....

....

....

♥ 16 ♥

WRITE REFINEMENT INTO YOUR LIFE

Anyone with a brush and a can of paint can create a painting. It's the same with sculpture, pottery, or other art forms. But what makes a masterpiece is the willingness of the artist to refine the art. It takes time, patience, and attention to detail. No matter what vision the artist sees in the final outcome, it takes precision to get there.

In the same way, each one of our lives is a spiritual work of art. God has a vision of what He has designed our character to be, and He uses life's circumstances to refine us.

Psalm 66:10–12 (NASB) says, "For You have tried us, O God; You have refined us as silver is refined. You brought us into the net; You laid an oppressive burden upon our loins. You made men ride over our heads; we went through fire and through water, yet You brought us out into a place of abundance."

Our refinement is a difficult process, one which takes self-discipline and perseverance, but the results are worth the price. Our character is refined with each battle we face: faith grows as we depend on God; courage grows as we face fears; compassion grows as we undergo suffering; contentment grows as luxuries are lost. Each and every trial we face is another stroke of the master artist.

Romans 5:3–5 (ESV) tells us to "rejoice in our sufferings" because "suffering produces endurance, and endurance produces character, and character produces hope, and hope does not put us to shame, because God's love has been poured into our hearts through the Holy Spirit who has been given to us."

Yes, your suffering may be painful, but there is nothing more beautiful than a heart that has been shaped by the Master.

Ephesians 2:10 (NLT) says, "For we are God's masterpiece. He has created us anew in Christ Jesus, so we can do the good things he planned for us long ago."

How is God using trials in your life to refine you into His masterpiece?

....

....

....

....

....

....

....

....

....

....

....

....

....

....

....

....

....

....

....

....

After Elisabeth Elliot's husband, Jim, was violently murdered by an Ecuadorian tribe, she later wrote in *Secure in the Everlasting Arms*, "Have we the humility to thank our Father for the gift of pain?"

What gifts of pain do you need to thank God for?

....
....
....
....
....
....
....
....
....
....
....
....
....
....
....
....
....
....
....
....
....
....
....
....
....
....

In Zechariah 13:9 (ESV), God says, "I will put this third into the fire, and refine them as one refines silver, and test them as gold is tested. They will call upon my name, and I will answer them. I will say, 'They are my people'; and they will say, 'The LORD is my God.'"

A refiner's fire doesn't destroy the precious metal—only its impurities.
What parts of your life would burn away under fire?
What parts would become more beautiful?

Meditate on 1 Peter 1:6–7 (NIV):

In all this you greatly rejoice, though now for a little while you may have had to suffer grief in all kinds of trials. These have come so that the proven genuineness of your faith—of greater worth than gold, which perishes even though refined by fire—may result in praise, glory and honor when Jesus Christ is revealed.

Journal your praises to God for the sufferings you've endured that have made you even more precious in His eyes.

....
....
....
....
....
....
....
....
....
....
....
....
....
....
....
....
....
....
....
....
....
....
....

In *Why? Trusting God When You Don't Understand*, Anne Graham Lotz wrote, "The kind of trust God wants us to have cannot be learned in comfort and ease."

What are some ways you can make your life a little less comfortable in order to experience the trust God wants you to have as He refines you?

....

....

....

....

....

....

....

....

....

....

....

....

....

....

....

....

....

....

....

....

Hannah was barren because "the LORD had closed her womb" (1 Samuel 1:5 NASB).
Hannah's husband's other wife, who had many children, scoffed and provoked Hannah
endlessly. But Hannah knew what to do: go to the temple of the Lord.
There, through her tears, she made a vow to God that if He would give her a son,
she would dedicate his life to the Lord's service. She prayed so hard that the priest thought
she was drunk! When she cleared up the misunderstanding, the priest blessed her request.
The next year, Hannah's son Samuel—one of the greatest prophets of Israel—was born.

What do you learn about refinement from Hannah's story?

Renee Swope said, "God uses life's detours to get us to a better destination, if we're willing to go a new direction."

What "detours" do you think God is using to refine you spiritually? What's stopping your willingness to head in a new direction?

In *From Fear to Love*, Ray and Nancy Kane wrote, "The trials in our life are like purifying gold. God uses these trials to allow those character issues that are blocking our ability to love to rise to the surface."

Journal your thanks to God for the many ways He has used circumstances in your life to make you a better person.

....
....
....
....
....
....
....
....
....
....
....
....
....
....
....
....
....
....
....
....
....
....

Read Hebrews 12:5–14.

How does this passage inspire your walk with God?
Journal your thoughts and feelings.

Gabriel proclaimed that Mary was "favored" by God (Luke 1:28 NLT). Elisabeth prophesied that Mary was "blessed. . .among women" (Luke 1:42 NASB). And Mary pronounced, "All generations will call me blessed" (Luke 1:48 NLT). But Simeon had a different prophecy for the gifted woman: "A sword will pierce through your own soul" (Luke 2:35 ESV). Although it may have been an honor to birth and rear Jesus, it was torture to watch Him abused and murdered.

The blessings of God don't always come in the package we want. The Sermon on the Mount in Matthew 5:1–12 (NIV) lists Jesus' idea of blessings:

> *Blessed are the poor in spirit. . . . Blessed are those who mourn. . . . Blessed are the meek. . . .*
> *Blessed are those who hunger and thirst for righteousness. . . . Blessed are the merciful. . . .*
> *Blessed are the pure in heart. . . . Blessed are the peacemakers. . . . Blessed are those who are*
> *persecuted because of righteousness. . . . Blessed are you when people insult you, persecute you*
> *and falsely say all kinds of evil against you because of me.*

The items on that list sound like tortures, not blessings! Here's the good news:

> *. . .for theirs is the kingdom of heaven. . . .for they will be comforted. . . .for they will inherit*
> *the earth. . . .for they will be filled. . . .for they will be shown mercy. . . .for they will see*
> *God. . . .for they will be called children of God. . . .for theirs is the kingdom of heaven. . . .*
> *Rejoice and be glad, because great is your reward in heaven.*

We always want the second half without the first, don't we? But blessings often come in disguise.

Even when no one else sees your suffering, the Lord is keeping a record of everything you have withstood for His sake. The sacrifices you make for the kingdom will be rewarded in the end.

Psalm 84:11 (ESV) says, "For the LORD God is a sun and shield; the LORD bestows favor and honor. No good thing does he withhold from those who walk uprightly."

Meditate on this verse and write what God reveals to you.

_____

_____

_____

_____

_____

_____

_____

_____

_____

_____

_____

_____

_____

_____

_____

_____

_____

_____

_____

_____

_____

_____

Consider the Beatitudes of Jesus in Matthew 5:1–12.

*How does your Christian walk compare
to the blessed life Jesus describes?*

....
....
....
....
....
....
....
....
....
....
....
....
....
....
....
....
....
....
....
....
....
....
....
....
....

Author Nancy Leigh DeMoss wrote in her book *Brokenness*, "Contrary to what we would expect, brokenness is the pathway to blessing! There are no alternate routes; there are no shortcuts. The very thing we dread and are tempted to resist is actually the means to God's greatest blessings in our lives."

What are the paths you have taken
through brokenness to receive blessing?

Ephesians 1:3 (ESV) says, "Blessed be the God and Father of our Lord Jesus Christ, who has blessed us in Christ with every spiritual blessing in the heavenly places."

What kinds of spiritual blessings have you received from God through difficult and easy circumstances?

God told Sarah's husband Abraham, "I will bless her and will surely give you a son by her. I will bless her so that she will be the mother of nations; kings of peoples will come from her" (Genesis 17:16 NIV). But God waited until Sarah was ninety years old to fulfill His promise!

How have you had to wait on God's promises in the past? How long did you wait? How can you trust God even while you wait for Him?

Proverbs 3:13 (ESV) says, "Blessed is the one who finds wisdom, and the one who gets understanding."

How do you think a woman can acquire wisdom and understanding? How have you gained these virtues in the past?

....
....
....
....
....
....
....
....
....
....
....
....
....
....
....
....
....
....
....
....
....
....

In the collection *Once a Day Everyday. . . For a Woman of Grace*, it is written, "Our blessings include life and health, family and friends, freedom and possessions—for starters. And, the gifts we receive from God are multiplied when we share them with others."[6]

Everything you have has been given to you for a reason.
The more you use your gifts for God, the more blessed you are.
How are you using your blessings to bless others?

[6] *Once a Day Everyday. . .For a Woman of Grace* (Freeman-Smith, 2012), Day 181.

Proverbs 31:28–29 (ESV) says, "Her children rise up and call her blessed; her husband also, and he praises her: 'Many women have done excellently, but you surpass them all.'"

Read the rest of Proverbs 31. Record why you think this woman was called blessed by her husband and children.

Helen Keller, in *Midstream: My Later Life*, wrote, "Observers in the full enjoyment of their bodily senses pity me, but it is because they do not see the golden chamber in my life where I dwell delighted; for, dark as my path may seem to them, I carry a magic light in my heart. Faith, the spiritual strong searchlight, illumines the way, and although sinister doubts may lurk in the shadow, I walk unafraid towards the Enchanted Wood where the foliage is always green, where joy abides, where nightingales nest and sing, and where life and death are one in the Presence of the Lord."

In blindness and deafness, Helen Keller found blessings.
How does her quote inspire you?

♥ 18 ♥
WRITE ACCEPTANCE INTO YOUR LIFE

Every woman goes through a time—during school days, marriage, childbirth and rearing, career changes, traumatic events—when she asks, "Who am I?" She can also go through multiple seasons—childhood, pre-puberty, puberty, pregnancy, menopause—when she asks, "Who am I *now*?"

As Christians, though, we women have an identity that never changes—one we can maintain through any of life's chaotic journeys. Isaiah 62:5 (ESV) paints this picture from God's heart: "As the bridegroom rejoices over the bride, so shall your God rejoice over you." Our everlasting identity as part of the church is being the Bride of Christ.

This life is our engagement period, and every trial and blessing is another stitch in the pure white gown in which we will present ourselves. Ephesians 5:25–27 (ESV) explains it this way: "Christ loved the church and gave himself up for her, that he might sanctify her, having cleansed her by the washing of water with the word, so that he might present the church to himself in splendor, without spot or wrinkle or any such thing, that she might be holy and without blemish." God has designed everything in your life—good and bad—to prepare you for the ultimate wedding.

The best part is that Jesus will never divorce or abandon His people. God said, "I will make with them an everlasting covenant, that I will not turn away from doing good to them" (Jeremiah 32:40 ESV).

You have been accepted by God just as you are. He created you for personal fellowship, and one day, He will live among His people. You will see Him face-to-face and feast at His table as a coheir with Christ. You are perfectly and unconditionally loved by God, not because of who you are, but because of who He is.

The book of Hosea is about a man who was called by God to marry a prostitute named Gomer. Hosea loved Gomer and cared for her, but she kept running away. Time and again Hosea went after Gomer and brought her home, and despite Gomer's rejection and disrespect, Hosea continued to pour out his love on her.

How is this like Christ's love for you as part of His church, His bride?

Ephesians 5:22–23 (NIV) compares a husband and Christ: "Wives, submit yourselves to your own husbands as you do to the Lord. For the husband is the head of the wife as Christ is the head of the church, his body, of which he is the Savior."

How does your submission as a wife or as another subordinate figure reflect your commitment to Christ?

Isaiah 54:5 (NLT) describes Christ, your Savior, as your husband: "For your Creator will be your husband; the LORD of Heaven's Armies is his name! He is your Redeemer, the Holy One of Israel, the God of all the earth."

How can you as part of the church, the bride of Christ, submit to Jesus as your husband?

Martin Luther (the leader of the Protestant Reformation) and his wife Katie had a marriage made in heaven. The two former Catholics supported each other in both public ministry and personal relationship. This was a marriage of love and acceptance. Katie cared for her husband through illness, persecution, and lots of travelling, always treating him with utmost respect, and he loved her for it.

How can you love your spouse with the same kind of unconditional acceptance? How can you show everyone in your life that kind of love? How does a good marriage reflect the love of Christ?

The Bible says, "Whatever is good and perfect is a gift coming down to us from God our Father, who created all the lights in the heavens. He never changes or casts a shifting shadow" (James 1:17 NLT).

How does God's unchanging character encourage you as you think about your identity in Him?

Meditate upon Romans 8:38–39 (NIV): "For I am convinced that neither death nor life, neither angels nor demons, neither the present nor the future, nor any powers, neither height nor depth, nor anything else in all creation, will be able to separate us from the love of God that is in Christ Jesus our Lord."

How does this encourage you?

God says, "Do not fear, for I have redeemed you; I have summoned you by name; you are mine" (Isaiah 43:1 NIV).

God knows you by name. You are His. God is personal, not a distant stranger. He knows all about your life—how you were once an enemy and are now welcome in His presence. Meditate on this concept, then journal whatever ideas, thoughts, or feelings come to mind.

Beth Moore wrote in her book *Believing God*, "I don't know a single person who truly seems to bear the mark of God's presence and power in his or her life who hasn't been asked by God to be obedient in a way that was dramatically painful." When you encounter difficult circumstances, you may think God has abandoned you, but the above quote (and many scriptures) suggest the exact opposite—when you belong to God, you will have trials.

How does this comfort you?

Ephesians 1:18–19 (NIV) says, "I pray that the eyes of your heart may be enlightened in order that you may know the hope to which he has called you, the riches of his glorious inheritance in his holy people, and his incomparably great power for us who believe."

Ask God to open your eyes to your identity in Him.
Journal whatever thoughts, scriptures, feelings, and ideas come to you.

• 19 •

WRITE TRUST INTO YOUR LIFE

Most of us have had to make numerous choices for which the outcome was unclear. In those times, you may feel like Lewis Carroll's Alice asking the Cheshire cat, "Which path should I take?" To which he replies, "That depends on where you are going." Alice says, "I don't know." And the cat answers, "Then it doesn't matter which way you go."

Thankfully, we have more than a cat to lead us. We have the all-knowing, sovereign Lord. We may not know where we're going, but He does! As long as we follow Him, we'll get where we need to go.

Ruth of Moab found herself in a moment of life-changing choice. Her husband, father-in-law, and brother-in-law were dead. Ruth's sister-in-law decided to go back to the pagans of Moab. Her mother-in-law Naomi headed for her homeland of Bethlehem. With whom would Ruth go?

Ruth didn't hesitate—her place was with Naomi and the people of God. "Where you go I will go, and where you stay I will stay. Your people will be my people and your God my God" (Ruth 1:16 NIV).

Ruth followed the Lord despite not knowing the outcome, and she was blessed. In Bethlehem, Ruth caught the attention of Boaz, who married her and accepted Naomi like family, and together Boaz and Ruth produced a lineage in the bloodline of Christ.

You can never choose the wrong way when you are following the Lord. Even when it seems a difficult path, it's always the best option in the end. Proverbs 16:3 (NIV) says, "Commit to the LORD whatever you do, and he will establish your plans." When you trust Him with everything you have, God will not fail to fulfill His promises of blessing in your life.

Proverbs 3:5 (ESV) says, "Trust in the LORD with all your heart, and do not lean on your own understanding."

You may have been taught your whole life to lean on your own wisdom and understanding, but God calls you to trust Him no matter how dire the circumstances may seem. Have you ever experienced this kind of trust in God? Is He asking you to trust Him in this way now?

Consider Psalm 37:5 (ESV): "Commit your way to the Lord; trust in him, and he will act."

What opportunities do you have to commit your ways to God?

....
....
....
....
....
....
....
....
....
....
....
....
....
....
....
....
....
....
....
....
....
....
....
....
....
....

In Exodus 1:15–21, the Egyptian king commanded two Hebrew midwives, Shiphrah and Puah, to kill the Hebrew boys as they were born. But the midwives trusted and feared God more than the king, so they lied to him, telling him the Hebrew women gave birth before they could arrive. As a result of their faithfulness to God, He "was good to the midwives" (Exodus 1:20 NLT).

Have you had to choose between obeying God and an earthly authority? If so, what course did you take? What are some ways this may happen in the future? How would you respond?

Anne Bradstreet was a Puritan poet. She penned these words after a terrible fire at her house:

And when I could no longer look
I blest His name that gave and took,
That laid my goods now in the dust.
Yea, so it was, and so 'twas just—
It was His own, it was not mine.
Far be it that I should repine.

It's hard to trust God in tragedies, but He is the only hope there is. How can you trust God through your personal losses?

....
....
....
....
....
....
....
....
....
....
....
....
....
....
....
....
....
....

Elizabeth George, in her book *Breaking the Worry Habit. . .Forever!: God's Plan for Lasting Peace of Mind*, wrote: "Replace worry with prayer. How do you do that? You make the decision to pray whenever you catch yourself worrying."

Do you worry or pray more? Let your times of worry trigger your dependence on God. Get on your knees before Him. As you see your prayers answered, your faith will grow. Write your reflections.

Romans 10:17 (ESV) says, "Faith comes from hearing, and hearing through the word of Christ."

If you are struggling to trust God, strengthen your faith by reading His Word. If you've never read the Bible, start with the book of John and make notes on the scriptures that strengthen your trust in the Father.

....
....
....
....
....
....
....
....
....
....
....
....
....
....
....
....
....
....
....
....
....
....
....

In John 14:1 (ESV), Jesus said, "Let not your hearts be troubled. Believe in God; believe also in me."

In what ways are you having difficulty trusting God?
How does this affect other relationships in your life?

Eliza M. Hickok wrote the following verses:

I know not by what methods rare,
But this I know: God answers prayer.
I know not if the blessing sought
Will come in just the guise I thought.
I leave my prayer to him alone
Whose will is wiser than my own.

How does this little poem inspire you to trust God?

....

....

....

....

....

....

....

....

....

....

....

....

....

....

....

....

....

....

In *Just Enough Light for the Step I'm On*, Stormie Omartian wrote, "God doesn't often reveal the details of where He's taking you because He wants you to trust Him every step of the way."

What has God revealed to you about trusting Him?

♥ 20 ♥
WRITE PASSION INTO YOUR LIFE

Do you know any sports fanatics? With a wardrobe of team shirts or stickers on their car, these people are easy to spot. Sports—the first thing they talk about and what they spend most of their time and money on—are their absolute passion!

Amanda Berry Smith was the same way about her passion—Jesus Christ. She was born a slave and freed at a young age. Amanda learned to work hard and became well-known as an excellent scrub woman. But while she worked, she prayed and witnessed, and her messages were so moving that she was asked to speak all over the South and eventually overseas. She became known as "God's Image Carved in Ebony."

Amanda's passion for Christ helped people see past all the social obstacles of her day because she lived what she preached. She was praised for her modest dress and behavior. First Corinthians 10:31 (NIV) tells us, "Whether you eat or drink or whatever you do, do it all for the glory of God." Amanda never did anything halfheartedly; she loved God with all her heart, soul, mind, and strength because He first loved her.

She described the day Jesus filled her heart: "Oh what glory filled my soul! The great vacuum in my soul began to fill up; it was like a pleasant draught of cool water, and I felt it. I wanted to shout glory to Jesus!"[7] Her words echoed the emotional cries of David in Psalm 63:1 (ESV): "O God, you are my God; earnestly I seek you; my soul thirsts for you; my flesh faints for you, as in a dry and weary land where there is no water."

May you be as desperate for the presence of God and as passionate about what He has done for you. He has given you love and grace when you deserved judgment. He has offered you the kingdom of heaven freely. How can you not center your life around your love for Him?

---

[7] https://www.wesleyanholinesswomenclergy.org/amanda-smiths-amazing-grace/

Jesus said, "Where your treasure is, there your heart will be also" (Matthew 6:21 ESV).

Describe the things in life that you are passionate about. On what do you spend most of your time and money? How does your relationship with God compare to your other passions? How much time do you spend on the works of the Holy Spirit? On reading the Word?

Moments before she accepted Christ, Amanda was riddled with doubts of worthiness. Preacher John Inskip cleared them up by looking directly at her and saying, "You don't need to fix any way for God to live in you; get God in you in all His fullness and He will live Himself."[8]

How does this clear up any doubts you may have about your own worthiness and thus increase your passion for Christ?

. . . .

. . . .

. . . .

. . . .

. . . .

. . . .

. . . .

. . . .

. . . .

. . . .

. . . .

. . . .

. . . .

. . . .

. . . .

. . . .

. . . .

. . . .

. . . .

. . . .

. . . .

. . . .

[8] https://www.wesleyanholinesswomenclergy.org/amanda-smiths-amazing-grace/

Romans 12:10–11 (NASB) says, "Be. . .fervent in spirit, serving the Lord." The word *fervent* means intense or passionate.

What can you do to strengthen your fervor for the works of God?

Hannah More was a famous poet and playwright in London and a member of high society, but she was also a devout Christian. Although Hannah was a talented writer, she felt unsure that she should be a part of such luxury amid so much world suffering. She decided that "the mischief arises not from our living in the world, but from the world living in us." After a short hiatus of searching her heart, she came back to playwriting with two goals: first, to educate aristocrats on the basics of scripture; and second, to encourage them to act on their faith. "Action is the life of virtue, and the world is the theater of action," she said.

How does Hannah's passion for ministry inspire you in your own career, calling, and duties?

Titus 2:14 (NASB) says Christ came to "purify for Himself a people for His own possession, zealous for good deeds."

You are one of those purified "people"— enthusiastic to be His hands and feet, living a life filled with good deeds—for which Christ gave up His life. How does this verse inspire you?

God gave Deborah the courage to engage in battle against Israel's enemies when God's men trembled in fear. In her song of victory, the passion-filled Deborah sang, "The villagers ceased in Israel; they ceased to be until I arose; I, Deborah, arose as a mother in Israel" (Judges 5:7 ESV).

How is God calling you to be a passion-filled "mother" in your community?

....

....

....

....

....

....

....

....

....

....

....

....

....

....

....

....

....

....

....

....

....

....

Psalm 73:25–26 (NLT) says, "Whom have I in heaven but you? I desire you more than anything on earth. My health may fail, and my spirit may grow weak, but God remains the strength of my heart; he is mine forever."

Write a prayer asking God to give you passion for Him throughout your life each day.

In Colossians 3:23 (NLT), Paul wrote, "Work willingly at whatever you do, as though you were working for the Lord rather than for people."

What are some different types of ministries that could reflect your passion for the Lord as you work for Him? What are the gifts and talents you have that can be used to pursue your passion for the kingdom?

In *Just Think*, Nancy Nordenson writes, "The mind in love with God is engaged with God's thoughts and ways, just as a lover is engaged with the words and actions of the beloved."

Do you personally know someone with a passionate love for Christ?
What kinds of qualities do you see in that person?
Which of those qualities would you like to adopt for yourself?

♥21♥

WRITE VICTORY INTO YOUR LIFE

Jim and Elisabeth Elliot were the Christian missionary dream couple. They were newlyweds and passionate about the Gospel. They prepared to translate the Bible for an unreached people and chose the dangerous Auca tribe in Ecuador. During Jim's and four other male missionaries' second encounter with the tribe, they were slaughtered. Elisabeth and the other widows stayed in Ecuador, ministered to their husbands' killers, and eventually saw the Christian conversion of the entire tribe.

Elisabeth wrote in *These Strange Ashes*, "Of one thing I am perfectly sure: God's story never ends with ashes." As tragic as the Auca story is, it allowed these women to show unconditional love and forgiveness, which was the key to the Auca people's salvation. Through tragedy, God brought victory. James 1:12 (NIV) says, "Blessed is the one who perseveres under trial because, having stood the test, that person will receive the crown of life that the Lord has promised to those who love him."

Victory in Christ can come through suffering or even death, but the sacrifice is worth the outcome. The spiritual victories are what matter, not the trophies of this world. "For our struggle is not against flesh and blood, but against the rulers, against the authorities, against the powers of this dark world and against the spiritual forces of evil in the heavenly places" (Ephesians 6:12 NIV).

You can't always see the battles you encounter. Yet you engage in combat every day—temptation, fear, insecurity. But the good news is that Christ has already overcome! You just have keep trusting Him and fighting. You know who wins in the end. So no matter how dire the circumstances seem, hang on! You're on the winning team!

First John 5:4 (NIV) says, "For everyone born of God overcomes the world. This is the victory that has overcome the world, even our faith."

How have you overcome the world through faith?

_____

_____

_____

_____

_____

_____

_____

_____

_____

_____

_____

_____

_____

_____

_____

_____

_____

_____

_____

_____

_____

_____

Read Romans 8:31–39.

*How does this passage encourage you
as an overcomer?*

Nino was a slave in AD 320. She was transported to Iberia, and while she was there she was noticed for her virtue and prayer life. Soon she was known for healing, so when the queen became ill, she sought the Christ follower, and Nino relieved the queen of her suffering. After the queen was converted, the king, who had experienced his own miracle, also became a Christian. Even though Nino was a slave, she was more than a conqueror—and later was made a saint!

How does Nino's life inspire you in your own victory?

....

....

....

....

....

....

....

....

....

....

....

....

....

....

....

....

....

....

Proverbs 21:31 (NIV) says, "The horse is made ready for the day of battle, but victory rests with the Lord."

How has God brought victory in your life through difficult circumstances?

Someone once said, "You can thank God for what is good; you can learn something or begin a task or finish a long-delayed piece of work. You can cheer a friend and share a neighbor's burden. You can forgive. You can go the second mile. You can look for the best and be your best and go to bed feeling that you have put into this day and got out of it as much as you possibly could."

How can you have these "little victories" in your life today?

....

....

....

....

....

....

....

....

....

....

....

....

....

....

....

....

....

....

....

....

....

It has been said that difficulties, failures, or challenges are stepping stones to success.

What "stepping stones" in your life have made you a better person? How did God use them to bring you to a deeper understanding of life?

. . . .

. . . .

. . . .

. . . .

. . . .

. . . .

. . . .

. . . .

. . . .

. . . .

. . . .

. . . .

. . . .

. . . .

. . . .

. . . .

. . . .

. . . .

. . . .

. . . .

. . . .

Meditate on "Who Walks the Word with Soul Awake" by Florence Earle Coates:

Who walks the world with soul awake
Finds beauty everywhere;
Though labor be his portion,
Though sorrow be his share,
He looks beyond obscuring clouds,
Sure that the light is there!
And if the ills of mortal life
Grown heavier to bear,
Doubt come with its perplexities
And whisper of despair,
He turns with love to suffering men—
And, lo! God, too, is there?

Journal whatever thoughts, feelings,
and ideas about victory in life this poem evokes.

....
....
....
....
....
....
....
....
....
....
....
....

In Psalm 20:7–8 (ESV), David writes, "Some trust in chariots and some in horses, but we trust in the name of the LORD our God. They collapse and fall, but we rise and stand upright."

Write a prayer asking God to show you the small victories along the way and to give you the stamina to hold on until you find your ultimate success.

Exodus 23:20 (NLT) says, "See, I am sending an angel before you to protect you on your journey and lead you safely to the place I have prepared for you."

Thank and praise God for the victories you have experienced in this life. Then thank and praise Him in faith for the victory you have yet to receive but that He has promised.

....

....

....

....

....

....

....

....

....

....

....

....

....

....

....

....

....

....

....

....

....

....

....

·22·

WRITE PATIENCE INTO YOUR LIFE

The protestor's sign read, "WE WANT PATIENCE! WHEN DO WE WANT IT? NOW!"

Few people want to wait for solutions; they want instant results. But the best things in life require patience. Bodybuilders can't produce muscle overnight. They must discipline themselves over time. Children who get everything they want lose character, much like Veruca Salt in *Willy Wonka and the Chocolate Factory*. She found that immediate satisfaction can lead to the dumpster (in her case, literally).

Waiting requires faith and trust, and that pleases God. If we got everything we wanted right away, we would have no appreciation for the gifts. We wouldn't know what it was like to live without blessings, so we certainly couldn't have a full understanding of God's generosity. We are to heed the words of Psalm 37:7, 9 (ESV): "Be still before the LORD and wait patiently for him; fret not yourself over the one who prospers in his way, over the man who carries out evil devices! . . . For the evildoers shall be cut off, but those who wait for the LORD shall inherit the land."

Susanna Wesley was a devoted mother of nineteen children. Her husband Samuel once said, "I wonder at your patience; you have told that child twenty times that same thing." To this she replied, "If I had satisfied myself by mentioning it only nineteen times, I should have lost all my labor. It was the twentieth time that crowned it." Oftentimes a woman may give up on the work before she has received the result, but it paid off for Susanna, who is remembered as the Mother of Methodism because of her two famous sons, John and Charles.

It's the struggle of patience that teaches you that you can trust God to keep His promises, a confidence that produces contentment even during hard times.

Joyce Meyer says, "Patience is not simply the ability to wait—it's how we behave while we're waiting."

How have you been behaving while waiting on God to fulfill His promises in your life?

....

....

....

....

....

....

....

....

....

....

....

....

....

....

....

....

....

....

....

....

....

First Timothy 6:11 (KJV) tells the reader to "follow after. . .patience." Other Bible versions say to pursue "endurance," "perseverance," "steadfastness," or "tolerance."

What are practical ways you can follow after or pursue patience in your life?

....

....

....

....

....

....

....

....

....

....

....

....

....

....

....

....

....

....

....

....

....

....

....

Psalm 25:10 (ESV) says, "All the paths of the LORD are steadfast love and faithfulness, for those who keep his covenant and his testimonies."

How has God healed you, met your needs, or comforted you in the past? What does this tell you about the character of God?

Romans 5:3–4 (NIV) says, "We also glory in our sufferings, because we know that suffering produces perseverance; perseverance, character; and character, hope."

How have you seen this pattern in your own life?

....
....
....
....
....
....
....
....
....
....
....
....
....
....
....
....
....
....
....
....
....
....
....
....

In *The Christian's Secret of a Happy Life*, Hannah Whitall Smith wrote, "There can be no trials in which God's will has not a place somewhere; and the soul has only to mount into His will as in a chariot, and it will find itself 'riding upon the heavens' with God in a way it had never dreamed could be."

Thanksgiving in the midst of waiting can focus our minds on the work of Christ in the midst of the trial. Make a list of all the things you are grateful for in the midst of your current challenges.

....

....

....

....

....

....

....

....

....

....

....

....

....

....

....

....

....

....

....

....

Jacob loved Rachel so much that he agreed to work seven years for her father without pay just for the right to marry her. The day after their wedding, in the twilight of the morning, Jacob discovered that he had been tricked into marrying Leah, Rachel's older (less attractive) sister. In a fight for love, Jacob agreed to work seven *more* years to marry Rachel—but he had to wait one more week to do so! Rachel had had to wait seven years plus an additional week—which must have felt like forever—to finally marry the man she loved.

Have you ever had to wait for something longer than you expected? How did God work in your life during that time?

. . . .

. . . .

. . . .

. . . .

. . . .

. . . .

. . . .

. . . .

. . . .

. . . .

. . . .

. . . .

. . . .

. . . .

. . . .

. . . .

. . . .

. . . .

Augustine's mother, Monica, was a devout Christian, but her son took after his pagan father. Monica diligently prayed for their wayward son, who often caused mischief and whose mistress bore him his own son when Augustine was but eighteen. Fifteen years later, her continuous prayers paid off when Augustine, now thirty-three years old, accepted Christ and eventually became a powerhouse theologian.

In what ways is God telling you not to give up in your prayer life?

Read these promises of God:

- Deuteronomy 31:6
- Isaiah 41:10
- Galatians 6:9
- Mark 10:27

How does each verse inspire you to remain patient?

....

....

....

....

....

....

....

....

....

....

....

....

....

....

....

....

....

....

....

....

....

....

Jeanne-Marie Guyon was a French mystic who practiced Quietism—getting quiet before God, putting herself and her own thoughts aside, and listening to His voice. In the 1600s, this was quite a controversial topic, so Jeanne-Marie was at times confined to a convent and even locked up in the Bastille. Even still, she kept sharing her insights through her writings.

How would you respond to such suffering?
What does Jeanne-Marie's patience teach you?

♥23♥

WRITE COURAGE INTO YOUR LIFE

When you think of courage, you might imagine a person with confidence and unwavering strength. But courage requires fear. A courageous person is one who continues to follow her convictions in spite of terror, anxiety, or social pressure.

Mary Lyon felt that it was her calling to help women receive a Christian-centered higher education. When churches refused to support her, she went door-to-door, taking donations until she had enough money to fund Mount Holyoke Female Seminary in Massachusetts. In 1837, the doors opened with eighty female students, and today about 2,200 women enroll every year.

Mary Lyon had an entire society to fight, but she believed a Christian woman should "go where no one else will go; do what no one else will do." She urged women, "Never be hasty to decide that you cannot do, because you have not physical or mental strength. Never say you have no faith or hope," but trust in God.

Proverbs 28:1 (ESV) says, "The wicked flee when no one pursues, but the righteous are bold as a lion." When we are following the will of God, we have no reason to cower and hide. We can speak with authority because the power does not come from our own hearts, but from our calling and the Word of God.

"If God is for us, who can be against us?" (Romans 8:31 ESV). There is no greater power than Jehovah—the Great I Am. Isaiah 41:10 (ESV) says, "Fear not, for I am with you; be not dismayed, for I am your God; I will strengthen you, I will help you, I will uphold you with my righteous right hand." When God calls you, He gives you exactly what you need to accomplish His will. Yes, there will be times of struggle, but when you make it through the valley of the trial, you will see that the Master was there all along, fulfilling His purposes as you took each step.

Jessie Frémont was the wife of John Frémont, a senator, explorer, and terrible financier. But Jesse kept the family together, proclaiming, "I am like a deeply built ship—I drive best under a strong wind."

What are the strong winds in your life? How can you turn your sails to use those winds for your faith and not against it?

Remember the words of Christ as He faced death in the garden of Gethsemane. "Father, if you are willing, take this cup from me; yet not my will, but yours be done" (Luke 22:42 NIV). Jesus was disturbed by what He faced, but He courageously cried out, "Not my will, but yours"!

How does Jesus' example inspire you to trust the will of God even when circumstances are intimidating?

Meditate on this scripture: "Have I not commanded you? Be strong and courageous. Do not be frightened, and do not be dismayed, for the Lord your God is with you wherever you go" (Joshua 1:9 ESV).

How does this assurance of God's presence with you—
no matter what the situation or where you are—increase your courage?

In *Traveling Mercies*, Anne Lamott wrote, "Courage is fear that has said its prayers."

Write about three courageous Christians in your life or ones that you've read about. What brave things have they done? What character qualities do they have in common?

....
....
....
....
....
....
....
....
....
....
....
....
....
....
....
....
....
....
....
....
....
....
....
....
....

Psalm 27:14 (ESV) says, "Wait for the LORD; be strong, and let your heart take courage; wait for the LORD!"

Why do you think it takes so much courage to wait on the Lord?
Write about a time when you had to wait on God.
How did He come through for you?

Elisabeth Elliot said, "Fear arises when we imagine that everything depends on us."

What worries haunt your imagination?
What scriptures bring you comfort,
reminding you that you can depend on God?

Philippians 4:13 (ESV) says, "I can do all things through him who strengthens me."

How does this scripture apply to your own life?

Read Ephesians 6:10–18, which talks about putting on the whole armor of God.

*How does this passage inspire
you to have courage?*

....

....

....

....

....

....

....

....

....

....

....

....

....

....

....

....

....

....

....

....

....

....

Missionary Amy Carmichael said, "If I am afraid to speak the truth, lest I lose affection, or lest the one concerned should say, 'You do not understand,' or because I fear to lose my reputation for kindness; if I put my own good name before the other's highest good, then I know nothing of Calvary love."

How do her words challenge the way you interact with others?

•24•

WRITE FAITHFULNESS INTO YOUR LIFE

God doesn't demand dramatic acts of service from His people. We don't have to lead megachurches or witness to great crowds. When we worship, no one but God need be a witness.

The Christian life is really one of daily obedience in the simple things—love your neighbor, go into your closet and pray, give generously and cheerfully. It's a progression of sanctification and sharing the love of God with those in your daily influence.

This concept was exemplified by Thérèse of Lisieux. She called it "the little way": serving God through seemingly insignificant acts of love. Thérèse aimed "not to do extraordinary things, but to do ordinary things extraordinarily well." Her ministry was so powerful that she inspired another famous Catholic, Mother Teresa, who took Thérèse's vision of "the little way" to the world.

This little-way principle is illustrated in the story of Jesus when He was surrounded by a huge crowd of hungry people. He told His disciples, "You give them something to eat" (Mark 6:37 NIV). But all the disciples had was five loaves and two fishes. Yet after giving what little they had to Jesus, He multiplied it and was able to feed over five thousand people—and they still ended up with "twelve basketfuls of broken pieces of bread and fish" leftover (Mark 6:43 NIV)!

You can only give what you have, even if it's a little. But you should give it all to God. Keep tithing even when it's only pennies; keep practicing hospitality even when the house is crowded. God knows how to feed thousands with just a few fish and loaves. He can multiply your faithfulness in the little things to minister to the world.

Read the story of the loaves and fish in Mark 6:30–44.

What do you learn about faithfulness
in the little things in this passage?

Paul encourages you to continue in your faithful walk with God, step-by-step, day by day. He serves as an example of what the Christian journey should look like: "Forgetting what lies behind and straining forward to what lies ahead, I press on toward the goal for the prize of the upward call of God in Christ Jesus" (Philippians 3:13–14 ESV).

What from your past is holding you back, and how can you let it go? How does Paul's imagery inspire you to keep working toward accomplishing God's will in your life?

Anna was a widow, prophetess, and faithful servant of God. Luke 2:37 (NIV) says, "She never left the temple but worshiped night and day, fasting and praying." Her faithfulness was rewarded at the age of eighty-four when she had the honor of bearing witness to the Christ child.

Faithfulness has rewards. How has this been true in your life and the lives of other Christians?

Joni Eareckson Tada said, "The Christian faith is meant to be lived moment by moment. It isn't some broad, general outline—it's a long walk with a real Person. Details count: passing thoughts, small sacrifices, a few encouraging words, little acts of kindness, brief victories over nagging sins."

Do you know Christian women that exemplify faithfulness in the little things? What qualities do you admire about them?

Mother Teresa dedicated her life to being faithful in the little things, to feeding the poor, to loving the unlovely. She said, "There are many people who can do big things, but there are few people who will do the small things."

What are the little things you can do faithfully at your church? At home? In your relationships with others as you interact with people day-to-day?

....
....
....
....
....
....
....
....
....
....
....
....
....
....
....
....
....
....
....
....
....
....

As a young girl, Mary of Nazareth was poor, humble, and simple, yet she was a faithful follower of Jehovah. In Luke 1:38 she describes herself as a "servant" or "slave" of God, ready to do His will. God could have chosen a queen or at the very least a woman from a wealthy family, but instead He chose a girl with little earthly possessions and a heart full of faithfulness.

Mary isn't known for anything except her duties as an ordinary housewife, mother, and faithful follower of God. How can you be faithful in your role as wife, mother, and/or mentor to other women?

Faithfulness is one of the fruits of the Spirit as described in Galatians 5:22–23.

What steps can you take to grow deeper in the Spirit so the fruit of faithfulness develops and flourishes?

....

....

....

....

....

....

....

....

....

....

....

....

....

....

....

....

....

....

....

....

....

....

In her book *Kept for the Master's Use*, Frances Ridley Havergal writes, "Again and again, God has shown that the influence of a very average life, when once really consecrated to Him, may outweigh that of almost any number of merely professing Christians."

How does this quote challenge you?

Read about Elijah and the widow of Zarephath in 1 Kings 17:7–24.

What are the little things God has given you to be faithful with?

•25•

WRITE FRUIT INTO YOUR LIFE

Adam named the woman God gave him Eve, which means "mother of all living." The couple was told to "be fruitful and multiply and fill the earth" (Genesis 1:28 ESV). Eve, literally the mother of all mothers, produced an entire race!

As Christians, we are also called to be mothers—spiritual mothers—and produce a family of believers. Jesus said, "By this my Father is glorified, that you bear much fruit and so prove to be my disciples" (John 15:8 ESV). Jesus uses the analogy of fruit to signify the life-giving nature of the Gospel. Just as a healthy vine produces beautiful grapes, the Word of Christ produces spiritual life.

Henrietta Mears is a prime example of spiritual mothering. After moving to Hollywood Presbyterian Church in Los Angeles in 1929, she attracted and worked with many young people from her church congregation as well as from local colleges, including UCLA. This was her goal in life: "Only the best possible is good enough for God." She personally led thousands to Christ, but she also mentored many young people through Bible studies.

Over the course of her ministry, over four hundred church and ministry leaders emerged, including Bill Bright, founder of Campus Crusade for Christ, and Billy Graham, who said, "I doubt if any other woman outside my wife and mother has had such a marked influence [on my life]. She is certainly one of the greatest Christians I have ever known."

Miss Mears's effectiveness came from her own relationship with God. She herself was deeply connected to the vine, and she joined people to the same source of life that she was attached to—the Word of God. Jesus said, "Whoever abides in me and I in him, he it is that bears much fruit, for apart from me you can do nothing" (John 15:5 ESV). Henrietta's success was no secret: love the Word with all your heart, and share it.

Susanna Wesley took her role as mother and spiritual mentor to her children very seriously. "I cannot but look upon every soul you [her husband] leave under my care as a talent committed to me under a trust by the great Lord of all the families both of heaven and earth." As she led her family in devotions, others visitors began to join, and soon two hundred or more were coming to Susanna's house to listen to her teach with zeal.

How does her example inspire you?

Galatians 5:22–23 (NLT) says, "The Holy Spirit produces this kind of fruit in our lives: love, joy, peace, patience, kindness, goodness, faithfulness, gentleness, and self-control."

Can you see any fruit from your own life? Who have you led to Christ? With whom have you shared your testimony? Who have you discipled? With whom have you touched with the fruit of the Spirit?

....

....

....

....

....

....

....

....

....

....

....

....

....

....

....

....

....

....

....

....

....

In John 15:4–5 (ESV), Jesus says, "Abide in me, and I in you. As the branch cannot bear fruit by itself, unless it abides in the vine, neither can you, unless you abide in me. I am the vine; you are the branches. Whoever abides in me and I in him, he it is that bears much fruit, for apart from me you can do nothing."

How are you connected to Jesus—the True Vine?

Corrie ten Boom said, "Trying to do the Lord's work in your own strength is the most confusing, exhausting, and tedious of all work. But when you are filled with the Holy Spirit, then the ministry of Jesus just flows out of you."

Write a prayer asking God to help you deepen your roots in him in order to produce good, free-flowing fruit.

....
....
....
....
....
....
....
....
....
....
....
....
....
....
....
....
....
....
....
....
....
....
....
....
....
....
....
....

The apostle Paul knew many women who supported his ministry—Lydia (see Acts 16:14), Phoebe (see Romans 16:1), Chloe (see 1 Corinthians 1:11), and Rufus's mother (see Romans 16:13).

*Whose ministry can you support with
your money, time, and prayer?*

....

....

....

....

....

....

....

....

....

....

....

....

....

....

....

....

....

....

....

....

....

....

....

In Matthew 7:17–19 (ESV), Jesus said, "Every healthy tree bears good fruit, but the diseased tree bears bad fruit. A healthy tree cannot bear bad fruit, nor can a diseased tree bear good fruit. Every tree that does not bear good fruit is cut down and thrown into the fire."

How does this scripture challenge you?

In Jeremiah 17:10 (ESV), God says, "I the LORD search the heart and test the mind, to give every man according to his ways, according to the fruit of his deeds."

What fruit does God find in your life?

Second Timothy 1:5 says that the faith that first lived in Timothy's grandmother Lois and his mother Eunice now lives in Timothy himself.

Think of three women in your life—relatives, church family members, friends, authors—who exhibit good fruits. What qualities do you admire about them? What makes them different? How does their faith and its fruits now dwell in you?

Ponder this poetic question from an unknown author:

If the whole world followed you,
Followed to the letter. . .
Tell me—if it followed you,
Would the world be better?

Ask God to show you how you can be more fruitful by abiding in Him and by continuing to write Him into your life.